Leila Pack

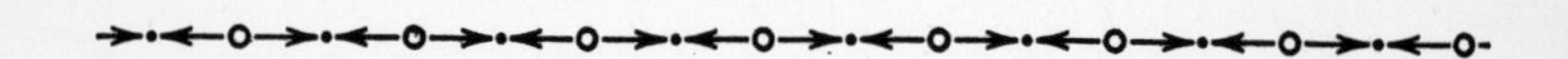

OTHER BOOKS BY NEWMAN LEVY

My Double Life
Opera Guyed
Theater Guyed
Gay but Wistful
Saturday to Monday
Twelve Hundred a Year (*with Edna Ferber*)

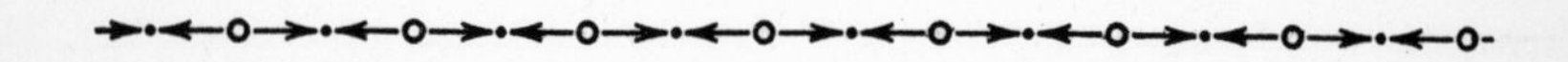

NEWMAN LEVY

The Nan Patterson Case

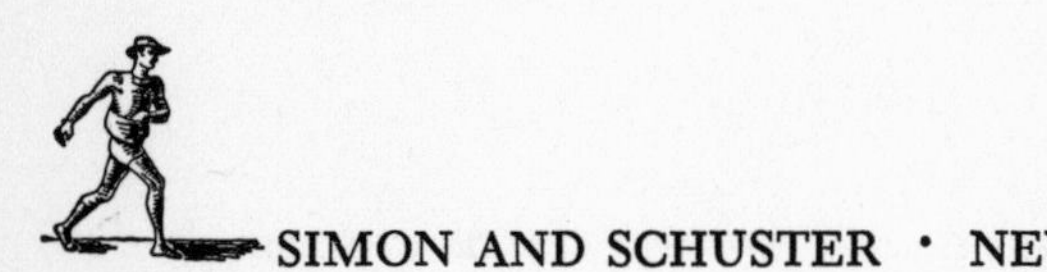

SIMON AND SCHUSTER · NEW YORK · 1959

PUBLISHED BY SIMON AND SCHUSTER, INC.
ROCKEFELLER CENTER, 630 FIFTH AVENUE
NEW YORK 20, N. Y.

FIRST PRINTING

LIBRARY OF CONGRESS CATALOG NUMBER: 59–7268

MANUFACTURED IN THE UNITED STATES OF AMERICA
BY AMERICAN BOOK–STRATFORD PRESS, NEW YORK, N.Y.

To the memory of a great lawyer,

my father

Contents

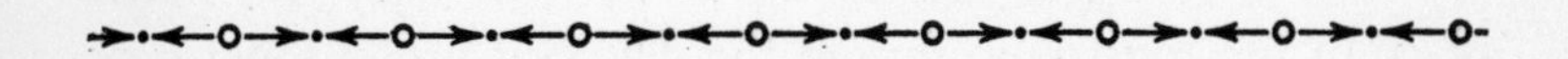

Author's Note

Abraham Levy, the lawyer who defended Nan Patterson, was my father. I was fifteen years old at the time, and the case was a momentous event in our household. My younger sisters had two kittens, one called Nan and the other Caesar. New York had many newspapers in those days. We got them all and I believe that I read every word that was printed about the case. Father tried many more important and more difficult cases during his long career at the bar but none that ever caused the excitement that Nan Patterson's did.

This is still a mystery story, and so I want to disabuse the reader of any idea that I have inside information about what really happened in that hansom cab. Father was a delightful raconteur, and frequently when he came home in the evening he would tell us—generally after one or two bourbon highballs—of amusing or interesting occurrences that had taken place in the courtroom during the day. But professional confidences were sacred. If he knew the secret of the Nan Patterson case, it died with him.

I must make it clear, therefore, that everything I have written in this book has been taken from the stenographic minutes of the trial and from yellowing newspaper accounts. Father used to keep scrapbooks of clippings about his cases, which I have. There are several thick volumes about Nan Patterson. I am grateful to my friend and former partner, Albert Blogg Unger, for lending me his father's scrapbooks. Judge Unger was Father's partner during the Nan Patterson case.

I am also fortunate to own what I believe is the only copy in existence of the stenographic minutes of the trial. The newspapers covered the case thoroughly, but there is much in the record that did not appear in the press.

I was tempted to use the semifictional method that many writers have employed successfully; but whatever might have been gained by way of artificial coloring, had I permitted myself to draw on my imagination, would certainly have made the reader justifiably wary of the authenticity of the book. The Nan Patterson case was one of the great murder trials in American criminal jurisprudence. I believed that it should be accurately reported.

NEWMAN LEVY

Westport, Connecticut

CHAPTER ONE

Death in a Hansom Cab

At about eight o'clock on the morning of June 4, 1904, a man and a woman stood at Columbus Circle near the entrance to Central Park. The man was well dressed except for a rather shabby black derby hat. The woman, who was noticeably attractive in the curvaceous fashion of the period, wore a violet walking suit and a light lavender-and-violet hat with a red rose on it, and in her hand she carried a pair of white gloves and a black handbag.

The man signaled to a hansom cab that was standing across the road at Eighth Avenue and Fifty-eighth Street. The cab, driven by Frederick Michaels, ambled over; the cabbie had been on a wild bender the night before and was not feeling quite alert.

The man assisted his companion into the hansom. "Drive

to West Fulton Street," he said, "and be there at nine o'clock. And stop on the way at a hat store."

The driver closed the doors of the cab and proceeded toward and then down Seventh Avenue at a leisurely trot. He drove through Twenty-fourth Street and stopped at Knox's hat store in the Fifth Avenue Hotel. The man jumped out of the cab. "This will do," he said. He went into the store and came out a few minutes later wearing a new hat. "Stop at a saloon on the way down," he told the driver as he got back into the cab.

They continued at the same leisurely pace along the cobblestones of Fifth Avenue, through Washington Park, and then down West Broadway. As they passed a saloon at the corner of Bleecker Street and West Broadway the man lifted the trap and ordered the driver to stop. He and his companion entered the saloon through what was chastely called, in those days, the "ladies' entrance" and remained long enough for a drink or two.

When they returned he again gallantly assisted his companion into the cab. "Drive to Fulton Street and be there at nine o'clock," he said. As they reached West Broadway and Franklin Street, Mr. Michaels heard the sharp report of a pistol inside his cab. This didn't bother the driver, but the shot appears to have startled his horse. "The horse started down," Michaels later testified, "and when I started to pull him up—I pulled him up and the lady raised the trap and told me to drive to a drugstore."

A young man named William Stemm, Jr., standing on the sidewalk, heard the shot and saw smoke coming from the cab. He ran after it and hopped on the back step.

At the drugstore the woman exclaimed to the driver,

"Hurry up and call that man out!" The druggist came out onto the sidewalk, and Mr. Michaels calmly explained to him that a man had been shot in his cab. The druggist directed him to the nearby Hudson Street Hospital. As the cab continued on its unhurried way, Officer William J. Junior, who was directing traffic nearby, stopped it and climbed up on the step. The cab driver swung open the doors, and there lay the man sprawled across his companion's lap with a bullet wound in his chest. By the time the cab reached the Hudson Street Hospital he was dead.

The man was Francis Thomas Young, known as Caesar Young, a nationally known gambler, bookmaker and racehorse owner. The woman was Nan Patterson, a onetime chorus girl who had recently been a member of a road-company *Floradora* sextette.

In those placid days at the beginning of the century, before two world wars and other earth-shaking events had preempted the front pages of the newspapers, journalism was somewhat less restrained than it has since become. William Randolph Hearst and Joseph Pulitzer were still engaged in their strident contest for circulation that gave birth to the phrase "yellow journalism." The Russo–Japanese War was raging abroad; Teddy Roosevelt in the White House was strenuously battling to bust the trusts; in June 1904 the steamship *General Slocum* burned in New York Harbor with the loss of over nine hundred people; on the sixteenth day of June 1904 Mr. Leopold Bloom took a memorable tour about the streets of Dublin.

But these events were quickly overshadowed in the newspapers by the strange mystery of the chorus girl who was accused of murdering a bookmaker. For almost two years scare headlines—they went in heavily for red ink in those days—were blazoned across the front pages of the papers not only in New York but throughout the United States. Battalions of reporters wrote millions of words; countless artists drew countless pictures; and sob sisters shed buckets of sentimental tears. It was a riotous journalistic jag, and the American newspapers have never had such a good time.

As the case progressed along its lurid way, legends grew up about Nan. At times it is difficult to separate truth from fiction, but certain facts concerning her history appear to be established.

At the time of the shooting, Nan, who had prosaically been christened Anna Eliza, was about twenty-one or -two years old. She had four sisters: May Queen, who was married to a man named Will Milburn; Mrs. Edward Taylor; Mrs. Harriet Lowell; and Julia, married to J. Morgan Smith. The Smiths will bear watching. They are important actors in this drama. The others may as well be forgotten now. Only May Queen will reappear in our story and that very briefly. There was also a younger brother, C. H. Patterson, a clerk in a Washington haberdashery shop. He may be forgotten too.

Nan's family was well-to-do. Her father, John B. Patterson, had been for many years supervising architect of the United States Treasury, a position he had patriotically resigned upon the election of Grover Cleveland because of his unwillingness to serve under a Democrat. He then engaged in the real-estate business in Washington, where he seems to have been prospering in the spring of 1904.

When Nan went on the stage she took her mother's maiden name and called herself Nan Randolph, which gave rise to the stories that began to be current about her aristocratic antecedents. On June 6, 1904, two days after the shooting, the New York *American* said:

> The interest in the case will be heightened by the knowledge that Nan Patterson, the girl now in the Tombs, is a great-granddaughter of John Randolph of Roanoke and the daughter of John B. Patterson who was for many years supervising architect of the United States Treasury Department. . . . One of her uncles was a United States Senator from New Hampshire. The young woman was splendidly educated in Washington where she lived until she came to New York a few years ago.

Whether or not Nan was an authentic Randolph of Virginia—she might indeed have been—is unimportant. The newspapers had discovered a heroine of the Southland, and henceforth, as the yellow press embraced her ecstatically, the story was drenched with the fragrance of jasmine and magnolia.

Nan Patterson was no raving beauty, but there is no doubt that she was a good-looking girl in the curved, buxom, high-pompadoured fashion that was the vogue in 1904. On the day after her arrest the New York *Herald* described her thus:

> Nan Patterson is a woman of more than ordinary attraction. Her hair, which is dark brown, was massed on the top of her head yesterday under a becoming hat with just enough color in it to make it noticeable. Her eyes are blue and her features are regular. When she was arrested her fingers were covered with rings, most of them of great value. She had a heavy gold chain around her neck and a diamond pin in her bosom.

The *Evening Telegram* said:

> Nan Patterson is apparently not more than twenty-five years old, with an abundance of brown hair. She has blue eyes and a fair complexion, is about five feet seven inches, and weighs 135 pounds. Her appearance is decidedly striking, and although she might not be termed beautiful she is a woman who would quickly attract attention and would be termed good looking.

This was how the reporters saw her in the police station and in court a few hours after Caesar Young had been shot, when she was undergoing an agonizing emotional experience. Throughout this story we meet her, for the most part, in the Tombs and in the courtroom when she was on trial for her life. There she was playing a most trying role, but we know that in her happier days, before tragedy descended upon her, she was gay, vivacious and fun-loving.

Nan strongly appealed to men, and her popularity did not entirely depend on her accommodating morality. She was not profound, but profundity was not a quality greatly in demand at Rector's and the race tracks. She was a good companion.*

In 1898, when Nan was sixteen years old, she was married to a young man named Leon Gaines Martin, with whom she came to New York to live. They had been together less than a year when Nan left him to join the chorus of a musical comedy. She had no talent, but she had other undoubted

* I saw Nan Patterson on two occasions. My recollection, which is not sharp after fifty-four years, is of a doll-faced, good-looking young woman—what W. S. Gilbert described as "a plump and pleasing person." It was in the courtroom and her face was pale, expressionless and impassive.

accomplishments that were quite as important to a successful career on Broadway. Not much was known about young Martin, but that didn't deter the fervid imagination of the press. Thus we read that he was the only son of wealthy parents, who, when Nan left him, bought him a seat on the New York Stock Exchange. But he could not be consoled for the loss of his young bride, so he sold his seat and joined Stuart Robson's Theatrical Company, about to go on a Western tour, in the hope that he might find Nan and bring about a reconciliation.

A more plausible story is the one in the *Times* of June 7, 1904, which stated that Martin had worked in the package room at the Baltimore and Ohio station. Later he obtained a railroad position and went to California. "He had but little money," the *Times* said, "and was unable to gratify his wife's expensive taste in dress."

Martin plays no important part in our story, but it is interesting to hear what he had to say about her introduction to the primrose path. "I feel responsible to a certain extent for the trouble of my former wife," he told a reporter. "I married her when she was scarcely more than a child. I brought her to New York and introduced her to a fast crowd of people. She was beautiful and strongly magnetic."

Nan may have been the demure Southern belle of romantic legend, but it did not take her long to grow accustomed to the ways of the wicked city. For this was the fabled, sparkling Gotham of a half century ago, the memory of which still moves old-timers to sentimental, nostalgic tears.

CHAPTER TWO

The Gay White Way

NEW YORK at the beginning of the century, or at least that section of it that forms the background of this story, was fascinatingly gay and extravagant. Great fortunes were being made and spent; it was an era of glittering, ostentatious living.

In the upper reaches of society, in that rarefied atmosphere that supposedly only four hundred persons were permitted to breathe, the bastions of exclusiveness were beginning to weaken. The elderly Mrs. Astor still ruled as the arbiter of fashion, but her long reign was drawing to a close and newcomers whose corpuscles were not certifiably blue were mingling strangely with the aristocracy. Artists, writers and, amazingly, even actors were becoming socially acceptable.

The ideal of masculine elegance in this period was the man about town as personified by the dashing author and war correspondent Richard Harding Davis and his handsome fictional hero, Van Bibber. This was the golden age of the matinee idol, and young women of all ages sighed and gushed over the virile charms of James K. Hackett, John Drew, Robert Edson and E. H. Sothern.

Feminine beauty was pictured in the luscious contours of Charles Dana Gibson's wasp-waisted ladies whose whalebone-encased figures and long, flowing skirts gave them the alluring walk and posture of stately camels. "Walk with a crick in your back and they'll call you a Gibson Girl," Valeska Suratt sang.

In the afternoon the fashionable world and those ambitious to be considered part of it would drive, richly attired, along the leafy drives of Central Park in handsome victorias and barouches drawn by high-stepping horses, with stately, liveried coachmen and footmen on the box. Tallyhos tooled down the country roads, their horns winding merrily, on their way to the races at Belmont and Sheepshead. In the winter the first snowfall would be welcomed by a stirring race of sleighs, their bells jingling, to the Central Park Casino to win the magnum of champagne that was given to the first arrival.

In those days it was the gracious custom, which still happily prevails, for men to forgather at the close of their day's labors at one of the popular bars for a cocktail or two—or possibly three or four. There one might see persons prominent in the world of finance, politics, gambling and the stage; one might mingle with characters notorious in the underworld, and, of course, with that indefinable multitude that just likes to drink in the afternoon.

One of the most popular of these oases was the Hoffman House Bar opposite Madison Square, where hung the famous nude painting by Bouguereau. A drawing of the period shows Grover Cleveland conversing affably at the bar with Chauncey M. Depew, while Tony Pastor, Nat Goodwin and Buffalo Bill stand nearby.

The gathering place for persons noted in the world of finance was the Men's Café in the recently built Waldorf Astoria. There one might occasionally see Judge Elbert H. Gary, that astonishing gambler-financier, John W. "Bet a Million" Gates, and even the mighty J. P. Morgan himself.

Afternoon drinking was, as yet, a masculine prerogative, but there were places, such as the café in Louis Martin's restaurant, that were hospitably open to ladies of unconventional habits if accompanied by escorts. It was said that an attractive, unaccompanied lady, afflicted with a late-afternoon thirst, had little difficulty in acquiring a companion.

Other favorite spots were the bars of the Gilsey House, Haan's on Herald Square, the Normandie, and George Considine's Metropole, popular with people of the theater and the sporting fraternity. When the afternoon libation was completed the man about town would hasten home to dress for dinner and the nightly ordeal of eating, drinking and being merry.

As night fell a glow would light up the sky along Broadway from Madison Square to Longacre Square—a luminous strip about a mile long. This was the fabled Gay White Way, the shrine and symbol of Gotham's wickedness, at which the rest of the country gazed disdainfully and enviously. It was here—or in its environs—that the man about town, gorgeously attired in top hat, white tie and tails, would arrive for dinner with an equally gorgeous, bejeweled and beplumed companion. Dinner might be at Shanley's or Bustanoby's Café des

Beaux Arts or Martin's. Or if the man about town particularly wanted to splurge it might be Delmonico's or Louis Sherry's new restaurant on Fifth Avenue.

Then to the theater. This was a vintage period in the theater and the fare was rich and varied. The theatergoer could, in 1904, have a choice that ranged from the inimitable buffoonery at Weber and Fields' Music Hall to Mrs. Fiske in *Hedda Gabler*. In that year one could have seen Richard Mansfield in *Ivan the Terrible*, Maude Adams in *The Pretty Sister of José*, James K. Hackett in *The Fortunes of the King*, Ethel Barrymore in *Sunday*, E. H. Sothern in *The Proud Prince*, Otis Skinner and Ada Rehan in *The Taming of the Shrew*, and many others.

When the curtain fell on the last act the audience would crowd out onto the sidewalk to await their broughams and cabs that were being called up by the doorman. The curtain inside the theater had fallen, but for the man about town the night was just beginning.

At the northern end of the Gay White Way, on the east side of Longacre Square between Forty-third and Forty-fourth streets, was Rector's. It was housed in a long, low yellow building and no name appeared outside to declare its identity. No name was needed. An electrically illuminated griffin hung above the entrance to proclaim that this was the legendary temple of Gotham's night life. To be seen and recognized at Rector's, to be privileged to sit at one of the tables on the main floor ordinarily reserved for Broadway's elite, was a social distinction beyond price.

By midnight each night the hundred tables downstairs and the seventy-five less distinguished tables upstairs were crowded. As one looked about the room one might see the debonair

John Drew; Charles Frohman, Broadway's most distinguished theatrical producer; Frankie Bailey, renowned for the incomparable symmetry of her legs; Florenz Ziegfeld, the future glorifier of American girlhood; and Ziegfeld's wife-to-be, the lustrous-eyed Anna Held, fresh and radiant from her much-publicized milk bath. One might also see, almost any night, glorious Lillian Russell, now somewhat past her prime and grown buxom after several marriages but still a glittering beauty. Miss Russell's escort was likely to be Diamond Jim Brady, mountainous and flashing like a display of fireworks.

James Buchanan Brady, who had amassed many millions as a salesman of railroad equipment and as a shrewd Wall Street speculator, was a triple-chinned Gargantua, weighing over two hundred and fifty pounds, celebrated for his millions, his gaudy collection of valuable jewelry and his incredibly enormous capacity for food.

Brady was said to own thirty sets of jewelry, each composed of twenty items that contained in all more than twenty thousand diamonds and over six thousand other precious jewels. But it was to his colossal appetite that he owed his chief fame. Brady neither smoked nor drank, but he would often consume four gallons of freshly squeezed orange juice at a meal. A typical dinner consisted of four dozen oysters, a dozen hard-shell crabs, six or seven lobsters, a large steak, a tray of French pastry and coffee.*

In addition to those celebrities who had arrived, there were nightly to be seen at Rector's many ambitious young women

* I am indebted to Lloyd Morris' delightful book, *Incredible New York*, for these statistics. I have read similar accounts elsewhere but I still can't believe it.

who were industriously striving to climb Broadway's ladder of success. One of them who might occasionally be seen there was an obscure but comely chorus girl named Nan Randolph who was soon to achieve some fame under the name of Nan Patterson.

CHAPTER THREE

"Tell Me, Pretty Maiden . . ."

THE MUSICAL COMEDY sensation at the beginning of the century was an importation from England called *Floradora.* It was not a particularly good show, but those of us who saw it at that time can still recall the sparkling music and the enchantment of Edna Wallace Hopper as Lady Hollyrood. *Floradora* had a delightful score by Leslie Stuart that made up for the banality of the book, and one number in particular that was responsible more than anything else for its spectacular success. This was the famous double sextette that today still survives as one of the unquestioned classics of the musical theater.

Across the stage, to the lilting rhythm of Stuart's entrance music, came six stately show girls, perhaps the most celebrated array of beauties ever assembled on one stage. Each one was five feet four inches tall and weighed one hundred and thirty pounds to the ounce. They wore frilly, pleated pink skirts, large, black, ostrich-plumed picture hats, and carried parasols.

From the opposite side came six handsome young men in gray cutaways and top hats. "Tell me, pretty maiden," the young men sang, "are there any more at home like you?" To which the girls, swishing their skirts and twirling their parasols, responded, "There are a few, kind sir, and pretty girls and proper too."

New York went mad over the Pretty Maidens. There were never fewer than six encores of the sextette. Prominent New Yorkers such as Frederick Gebhard, the financier, and Stanford White, the city's most noted architect, reserved orchestra seats for every performance, arriving at the beginning of the sextette and leaving right after its conclusion. We may wonder if White didn't occasionally remain for the rest of the performance, for in the chorus of *Floradora* was a beautiful, dark-eyed girl named Evelyn Nesbit, who was later to play an important role in the architect's life. It would be interesting to know if Stanford White ever noticed her as she danced demurely in the chorus.

The original Pretty Maidens quickly became the toast of the town. At Rector's they exceeded in popularity the most noted stars of the day. They were deluged with flowers, gifts and stock market tips from their wealthy admirers, and several amassed substantial fortunes that enabled them to retire from the stage in affluence. Several of them married millionaires.

Floradora opened in New York at the Casino on November 11, 1900, and ran for 505 performances, which was a phenomenal run in those days. Then it went on the road and toured the country for years. Besides the original Casino company there were numerous road companies.

One of them, playing in California, was a troupe under the management of a man named Fred Herr, known in theatrical circles as Ben Herr, and in the chorus was Nan Patterson. One of the Pretty Maidens became ill and had to leave the show, and Nan was promoted to take her place in the sextette.

It was said later that her good fortune was due not so much to her theatrical ability as to the fact that Fred Herr had fallen desperately in love with her and had left his wife on her account. It was rumored at the time that Mrs. Herr had attempted to commit suicide because of her husband's desertion.

The company ran into financial difficulties and, as Herr remained behind in California to battle the sheriff and attachments, Nan took a train to New York. There she was promptly hired by the Shuberts as a chorus girl in *A Chinese Honeymoon,* which was in rehearsal at the Casino. She appeared in one performance. As she returned to her dressing room at the end of an act, she found a telegram from Fred Herr summoning her to join him in San Francisco.

The next day she was aboard a train bound west, and on the train, according to Nan's testimony at her trial, she met Caesar Young.

Fred Herr, to whom she was hastening for a reunion, was promptly forgotten, and by the time the train reached California Nan and Young were fast friends. There was a story, probably apocryphal, that poor Herr became insane from grief and committed suicide in Nan's presence. At any rate her intimacy with Caesar Young—which began early in 1903—quickly ripened into a mutual infatuation. They were seen together constantly at the races and it was not long before they were living together openly and notoriously.

CHAPTER FOUR

Caesar Young

FRANCIS THOMAS YOUNG had been famous in his younger days in England as a long-distance and cross-country runner. The Manhattan A. C., which was engaged in a keen athletic rivalry with the New York A. C., had brought him to New York and had established him luxuriously with free room and board at the clubhouse, and to preserve his amateur standing had given him a job in the office at a comfortable salary. He continued in this country the track victories he had won in England, the triumphs for which he had been nicknamed Caesar.

One day, as he was standing on the steps of the clubhouse watching the Decoration Day parade, a young woman in the crowd fainted. Young carried her into the club, where she was revived, and later took her home. She was Miss Margaret Becker, a beautiful girl of eighteen. He continued to see her frequently thereafter; the friendship developed into a romantic love affair, and before long they were married. At the time of Young's death they had been married twelve years.

Shortly after their wedding the Manhattan A. C. became involved in financial difficulties and had to close its doors. Young was out of a job, and he and his young wife were desperately hard up—so hard up that he took a job with the Western Union Telegraph Company in Brooklyn at ten dollars a week, supervising the messenger boys.

This job did not last long. Young was, by nature, a gambler, and to supplement his meager income he began to play the races. But his interest in racing was something more than a mere desire to make money; he had a genuine affection for horses and an inborn understanding of them. Soon he began to attract attention for both his daring and his uncanny gift for picking winners.

He had now found an occupation for which he had a real talent. One of the most prominent figures in gambling circles was a man named James Mahoney, who owned a chain of prosperous poolrooms and who was known as the "Poolroom King." He was impressed by Young's ability and offered him a position in charge of several of his poolrooms. A poolroom, the young reader should be informed, was a place where off-the-track betting on horse races was indulged in. It was an institution that flourished in an earlier, more liberal age. Here Young's knowledge of the racing game quickly manifested itself and the money began to pour in.

Before long he had accumulated a bank roll of seven thousand dollars and he decided to leave Mahoney and go in business for himself. He invested thirty-four hundred dollars in a horse and spent the balance of his money in training him. Unfortunately, just before the horse was to make its debut, it developed catarrhal fever and died.

Young was flat broke again, so he went back to Jim Mahoney, who put him in charge of one of his biggest poolrooms on the Upper West Side. Here he repeated his former success and soon he had accumulated another substantial bank roll.

Once more he resigned from Mahoney's to gamble on his own. He quickly became a well-known figure at the Eastern tracks from New Orleans to Sheepshead Bay and his success in picking winners became legendary. About 1899 he decided to become a bookmaker himself, to the great relief of the bookmaking fraternity who had been paying him vast sums of money.

He was even more successful as a bookmaker than "on the ground," and it was not long before he was beginning to train and race his own horses. In this enterprise his wife, who shared her husband's enthusiasm for racing, was his partner and assistant. Contemporary accounts state that Mrs. Young was the "businessman" of the firm.

In 1901 Young bought two mares for two thousand dollars. One was a horse named Eonic to which his wife had taken a fancy and which she trained herself. Eonic was entered in the Burns Handicap, the big racing event on the West Coast. The mare was unknown and the odds quoted against her were fifty to one. Eonic won easily and Young collected the $10,000 stake, which was a large purse fifty or sixty years ago. Mrs. Young, who had unbounded confidence in her horse, had bet heavily and was said to have won over $30,000.

Caesar Young was now rich, or rather his wife was, for most

of his wealth was shrewdly invested in her name. He bought a handsome home in Berkeley, a ranch in Sacramento, and a breeding farm in the same place. He also began to acquire valuable real estate in New York and California. At the time of his death he was worth well over half a million dollars.

Young was a lavish spender and a prodigious drinker. Throughout the records of the trial there is ample testimony to his remarkable capacity for drinking. We can gather from the evidence that Nan, too, was far from abstemious, and that her elastic moral code accommodated itself comfortably to Caesar's habits. For about a year and a half they followed the racing meets from Seattle to Los Angeles, betting heavily, living in the best hotels, and eating and drinking extravagantly.

Meanwhile Mrs. Young, who had contributed so much to her husband's career, was living unhappily alone in her expensive mansion in Berkeley, ignored and humiliated. Of course she soon knew of Caesar's affair with Nan; she testified in court that she had learned about it early in 1903. It was common gossip in sporting circles. Nan, who had been separated from her husband, Martin, obtained a divorce from him in the spring of 1903 at the urging of Young, who paid all the expenses.

Caesar Young's racing partner and closest friend was John D. Millin, a husky, ruddy-faced former prize fighter. Young had taken him under his wing and had shared his success with him, all of which Millin repaid with almost doglike devotion and loyalty. He was equally devoted to Young's wife, and he was outraged at his partner's treatment of her. His indignation was undoubtedly augmented by the fact that Young's notorious affair was doing his reputation harm and hurting business.

Millin believed that his partner was the innocent victim of a mercenary, designing woman, and his feelings hardened into a bitter hatred for Nan Patterson.

Millin had Young and Nan carefully watched, and their behavior and plans were duly reported to him. In the winter of 1903 he learned that they were about to elope to Washington, D. C. Together with Mrs. Young he followed them and they came face to face on the platform of the Los Angeles station as the eloping pair was about to board a train for the East.

An angry quarrel ensued as Millin tried to persuade his partner to return home, but Young stubbornly refused. Then Millin remembered a method of persuasion he had learned in his younger days. He hauled off and landed a terrific right-hander on Young's jaw. Caesar went out cold, and it took several hours to revive him. When at last he was able to sit up, he meekly consented to return to San Francisco. The elopement was broken up, but only temporarily.

In February 1904 the following item appeared in the *Morning Telegraph*, New York's sporting newspaper:

> *San Francisco*, Feb. 29—Racing circles were greatly surprised today over the disappearance of Bookmaker Caesar Young who eloped with Nan E. Randolph, one of the *Floradora* sextette girls. Young who has been drinking heavily for several days leaves a wife behind him. He has been infatuated with the Randolph woman for many months, and has spent large sums of money upon her. He left a letter for his wife saying he would marry Miss Randolph if he had to go to South Africa to do it. It is said that he took about $5,000 with him when he fled.

Young, presumably, had waited long enough for his aching jaw to heal and then had hastened to rejoin Nan in Los Angeles. There seems to be no doubt that he was madly in love with her.

The reunion in Los Angeles was copiously saturated with alcohol, and when the indomitable Millin finally tracked them down, he found them at eleven in the morning, sleeping off a jag in what Alexander Woollcott, writing about the case, described as "a singularly liberal-minded Turkish bath."

Again Millin employed his power of persuasion, but this time he did not have to use his fists. He told them that Mrs. Young was on her way to Los Angeles and that it would be well for Nan to get out of town. There were intimations that the long-suffering wife was on the warpath and there would be a devil of a row.

"You will have to leave. I'm in a fine fix," Young protested to Nan. "At least, clear out till this blows over."

"I suppose I will have to go if you want me to," Nan replied obediently.

Young's apparently meek surrender may come as a surprise, and it can be doubted if he really expected his separation from Nan to be of long duration. It was good policy to be acquiescent temporarily, for his wife had a powerful weapon if she cared to use it. It will be remembered that most of his wealth was in her name and she held the purse strings.

Moreover, Caesar, for all his bluster, was a weak man and essentially a man of peace. It was satisfying to have an attractive mistress and a pleasant wife and home—when it suited him to want them. It was annoying to have this charming arrangement threatened.

Millin, at Young's direction, bought Nan a one-way ticket, gave her, he said, eight hundred dollars (Nan subsequently testified that it was twenty-eight hundred dollars) and on March 2, 1904, put her on the train for New York. When she arrived she went to the apartment of her sister Julia, who lived with her husband, J. Morgan Smith, at 101 West 61st Street. There she remained for a brief visit and then went to Washington to see her parents.

Meanwhile the Youngs, to the delight of the faithful Millin, were apparently reconciled. Caesar was anxious to return East in time for the racing season which was approaching, and they planned to leave California, although the fact that Nan was in New York no doubt caused his wife and partner some misgivings. On April 21, Mrs. Young, accompanied by two young nephews, who had spent the winter with her, and Millin left San Francisco, and Young joined them on the train at Sacramento.

Everything was serene—at least on the surface—and if Mrs. Young was suspicious there is nothing in the record to indicate it, even when Young informed her with his characteristic abruptness that he had to stop off at Chicago on business but would meet her in New York in a few days. He left the train at Chicago, and his wife, Millin and the nephews continued on to New York without him.

The explanation of this strange conduct of a repentant husband can be found in Nan's direct examination at her trial.

Q. When you came back East in April where did you go?

A. I spent a night with my sister Julia who is Mrs. Morgan Smith, and then went to the home of my parents in Washington. I was with Mr. Young three or four days, and then went to Chicago where I waited for him by agreement. We were at the Wellington Hotel for several days when I went to Washington again.

Q. When you and Young were apart did you communicate by any means?

A. We wrote and telegraphed to each other constantly.

We can assume that during the romantic stopover in Chicago there were occasional interludes in the luxurious bedroom of the Hotel Wellington that were devoted to conversation. The situation was scarcely propitious for serious discussion, but Nan sensed that her hold upon her attractive, generous lover was weakening. His long-promised divorce was as far off as ever and she had the frightening realization that when he arrived in New York in a few days he would, after a year and a half, again be living with his wife.

Nan pleaded with him to hasten the divorce and Caesar, as was his habit, kept reassuring her that everything would be all right if she would be patient only a little while longer. Meanwhile it was important, he told her, to keep Mrs. Young and Millin in good humor.

Perhaps, under the euphoric effects of many bottles of champagne, Nan was partly convinced, but when they boarded the train for Washington—Caesar accompanied her as far as Harrisburg—she had an ominous foreboding that the end was drawing near. In Washington Young's letters, pressing her to stay away from New York, increased her fears. Clearly it was urgent that something be done. Disregarding his injunction, she boarded a train and, accompanied by her sister May Queen, she arrived in New York on the night of May second. The overture to the tragedy had begun.

Young arrived in New York on April twenty-ninth at the Hotel Walcott, where Millin had deposited Mrs. Young.

Some of his letters to Nan during this interval went into evidence at the trial. They are not fulsome love letters—one could hardly expect literary eloquence from an uneducated bookmaker; but they throw some light upon the relationship between the two. For the most part they are filled with gossip about horses and people whose names no longer have meaning after a lapse of more than half a century. A few excerpts will suffice.

". . . Princess doing fine," he wrote on May first, "won 100 at the races. Not so bad for a greenhorn. Suppose you wait till I send for you. Is May [presumably Nan's sister, Mrs. Milburn] coming? And where are you going? Love and kisses—Frank."

On May second he wrote, "Did not get home from New Rochelle until past eleven last night, went around to the Imperial and found your telegram and also letter. [They had arranged for her to send mail to the Hotel Imperial, not the Walcott where he was living.] Answered right away . . . For goodness sake, dear, don't telegraph me to meet you and be disappointed if I don't . . . You know, Nan, I have to win a big bet this summer, not only for myself, but for you, you understand, don't you?"

Nan did not wait for him to send for her. On May third he wrote to her again, but she had already arrived in New York. ". . . it seems to me you are having too many of those bottles, Nan, every letter I get there is a bottle in it and just going to get another . . . Hope you are not being sick, got to go to the track now, Nan, there were four men blackballed me in the Mets, there were eighty voted, one of them got up and made a speech saying that any man that would do what I did, and then he read the San Francisco paper, was not a fit person to belong to such an august body. Goodbye, Nan, love and kisses—Frank."

Young was clearly unhappy at this time with Nan pressing him on the one hand and his wife on the other. If only these women would leave him in peace! And then, to have been blackballed by the Metropolitan Turf Association, the exclusive organization of turfmen, because of his notorious affair with Nan, was an additional humiliation. If he could persuade her to stay away from New York for a while the impending storm would blow over and he could resume his pleasant, self-indulgent life. But Nan refused to be persuaded. She arrived with May Queen at the Pennsylvania Station and they took a cab directly to the home of Julia and Morgan Smith. After an emotional reunion, during which Julia told her some news that augmented her fears, Nan, in a state of great agitation, went over to the Hotel Navarre and took a room.

CHAPTER FIVE

Julia Writes a Letter

A FEW DAYS before Nan arrived in New York her sister Julia had dinner with a man named Coggins, a friend of Young's, who told her that Caesar not only had no intention of marrying Nan, but that he never had had any such intention. This conversation Julia repeated to her sister upon her arrival at her apartment in New York.

The next day at about eleven Julia visited Nan at her room in the Hotel Navarre. The other sister, May Queen, was there. Nan was "in an intensely excited condition," Mrs. Smith testified, "crying so you would call it hysteria . . . She had been crying very much apparently, from the appearance of her eyes, and she seemed quite agitated, and after I came in we talked for a few minutes and she began crying again, and of course then we had quite a long conversation and I understood the cause."

The cause of Nan's agitation, Julia explained, was that

Young's promised marriage to her had been indefinitely postponed. Under examination by Assistant District Attorney Rand, Mrs. Smith testified:

Q. That it had been postponed, not because of any failing of affection on the part of Young, is that right?
A. Yes, sir.
Q. But because Mr. Young's wife would not consent to divorce him?
A. Well, because of difficulties that had arisen.
Q. Did she say what the difficulties were?
A. That great influence had been brought to bear upon Mr. Young to prevent his getting a divorce, and I understood her to mean his wife and Mr. Millin.

The three sisters had lunch together at a nearby restaurant and then returned to the Navarre. Young had told Julia many times that he intended to marry Nan as soon as his wife consented to a divorce, and in the spring of 1903, when Julia was visiting her sister in California and Nan's divorce suit was pending, Young had said, "My proceedings have been begun, and I'm afraid—I think that unless you girls hurry my divorce will be granted before Nan's."

Nan's hysterics continued after lunch and she sobbingly declared that she was sure Young loved her, and she didn't believe a word that Coggins had said. May Queen took Julia aside and whispered that she was worried about Nan's condition and there was no telling what she might do, so Julia went downstairs and wrote a note to Young which she dispatched by messenger.

Young was not at home when the note arrived, but unfortunately Mrs. Young was. She opened it and read it, and then endorsed her name on the envelope. When her husband returned in the afternoon she gave it to him. We are not informed of what occurred on this occasion, but we can be sure that Mrs. Young, who was a woman of spirit, did not take lightly this documentary proof that Young's affair with Nan was still very much alive.

Julia Smith's note to Young was the object of violent legal battles at Nan's trial. Assistant District Attorney Rand considered it one of his strongest pieces of proof and contended that the letter indicated that even at this time Nan had homicide in her heart. This is what Julia wrote:

MY DEAR NUNC,

Can't you come up and see me at once. I am living at No. 106 West 61st St.*—the sixth floor, east side apartment. Nan has been with me since Monday when she left her mother accompanied by my sister, May Queen, who, fearing in her perturbed condition that she might do something either serious to you or herself, came to New York. I should like to get the whole thing straightened out and understand what is what. Mr. Coggins dined with Mr. Smith and myself on Sunday and said so much that I know cannot be true and which has made me most unhappy, and which has, under the present circumstances made Nan so unhappy, that she cannot bear it. I understand what the matter is and want you to do what is right at once. Either write to Nan or see me at your earliest convenience. You know that I love Nan better than anything on earth and she loves you above and beyond everything. To see her absolutely wild, as she is, breaks my heart. You must come and see me and get the whole matter straightened out. I shall expect you tomorrow before* 12 *o'clock.*

JULE

Young did not visit Julia the next day; instead, on the evening of the receipt of the note, he called on Nan at the Navarre. Morgan Smith and Julia were there and Smith, Nan said, "was drinking champagne and somewhat noisy."

Nan, under cross-examination by Rand, added some illuminating details of what took place at the Navarre that night:

Q. While at the hotel on the evening of May third, did Mrs. Smith faint?
A. She did.
Q. She fell on the floor?
A. Yes.
Q. What caused her to faint?
A. Her husband had been drinking.
Q. He was intoxicated and caused her to faint?
A. Yes.
Q. When did you first meet Morgan Smith?
A. Last March.
Q. Was he habitually used to liquor?
A. He had been. When he was intoxicated he used to get his jaw twisted. After a few drinks he would become rigid.
Q. He made such a disturbance that the house detective came up?
A. Some man came up. I don't know who he was.

Evidently the atmosphere that evening at the hotel was hardly suitable for an affectionate reconciliation. Nan and Caesar wanted to be alone, so they went out and took a drive through the park in one of those hansom cabs that play such a prominent part in this story. It was not quite as spacious as the room at the Hotel Wellington but it served its purpose. They remained out until about one o'clock in the morning.

Apparently they patched up their differences. Young declared fervently that what Coggins had said was not true and repeated that if she was patient Mrs. Young would eventually consent to a divorce. Nan was reassured, for on the following day, Julia said, she was her old, gay, cheerful self. A few days later she moved to the Hotel Imperial, where Young had taken a room for the two of them, registering under the name of "J. B. Patterson and Wife."

The state of Young's mind at this time was probably as Nan's counsel, Abraham Levy, described it in his summation to the jury. "I myself believe, if I may be permitted to say it, that the man never intended to get a divorce from his wife. I do believe that he misled the girl into the belief that he intended to do so. I believe that she believed he was going to get a divorce."

Young must have been kept pretty busy shuttling between the Walcott, where he was living with his wife, and the Imperial, where he was living with Nan. The Morgan Smiths were quite at home at the Imperial, visiting there daily, and on one occasion Millin, despite his disapproval of Nan, called there and participated in a convivial party. Young fell asleep on the bed and Morgan Smith, doing the honors, sent out for beer.

CHAPTER SIX

"...Were the Other Dear Charmer Away"

On the surface harmony appears to have been restored, but poor Caesar, between the pressures at the Walcott and the Imperial, was a harassed man. He could have been quite happy were the other dear charmer away. Perhaps Nan might like a trip abroad. To assist him in accomplishing this most delightful solution he enlisted the services of his brother-in-law, Bernard F. McKean.

McKean had married Mrs. Young's sister and was on friendly terms with Caesar. It may seem odd that Young should have drafted the services of a member of his wife's family, but the affair now was so notorious that there was no reason for concealment.

On Friday, May sixth, at about 10:30 in the morning Mc-

Kean and Young called for Nan in a hansom cab. This was the first time McKean had ever met her, and after Young had introduced them they drove uptown to Reisenweber's Café at Fifty-ninth Street, Nan sitting on Young's lap. This, as McKean told it in court, is what took place:

They sat down at a table, Young ordered a bottle of champagne, and then said, "Nan, I have brought you here to arrange the details of sending you to London, because I have to do so on account of Mrs. Young making more or less trouble for me. He [referring to McKean] will arrange all the necessary details, and will give you money from time to time as you may want it, and I want you to go tomorrow."

"No," Nan replied, "I cannot go tomorrow because I am having a couple of dresses made, and they will not be ready before Tuesday next."

"Well," Young said, "I would rather have you go tomorrow, but if you can't get ready you'll have to take the first boat sailing after you are ready."

They sent out for a newspaper and found that the *Teutonic* was sailing the following Wednesday. Young directed McKean to engage a stateroom for Nan and to arrange to send her baggage to the ship.

Nan protested. "I don't want to go!" she said. "I don't feel that I can leave you. If you would go with me and we could jump off the boat together and die in each other's arms I would be very happy and willing to go."

But Young kept insisting that she had to go. "Now, Caesar," Nan replied, "you have said that to me fifty times. Don't tell me any more that I have to go. Say you want me to go."

"Well," Young asked, "will you go?"

"Yes, I will," she replied.

"You know, Nan," Young said, "you always said you would go away if Mrs. Young ever made it necessary. Now I want you to make good because I am in trouble with her, and I know it will all be settled if you go away. I brought Barney along with me and if he tells Mrs. Young that you have gone away then everything will be very pleasant with me and she will believe it."

Nan continued to protest but she said she would go if he insisted. "If Julia hadn't sent that letter to me so that Mrs. Young would receive it," Young said, "I don't think you would have had to go away at all. You remember me showing you that letter, and showing you where Mrs. Young had signed it as opened by her and that she received the letter and turned it over to me. That brought on the trouble right away, almost the day I arrived in New York."

Young, with the querulousness of a man who was accustomed to having his own way, was trying to relieve himself of the embarrassment of Nan's presence. But Nan, on the other hand, was fighting desperately to hold on to her lover. Whether she actually was passionately in love with him may be questioned, but he was rich and companionable, and he represented to her security and a way of life that she had learned to enjoy thoroughly. And she knew well the strong physical attraction she had for him. At this point she played what she naïvely believed was her trump card.

"I'm four months pregnant," she said, and we can almost hear the tremolo in her voice. "My shape has altered and that's why I can't leave before I get my new dresses."

We have only McKean's word for it that this was said, but it has the ring of authenticity. Nan was a shrewd and intelligent girl, but addicted, as we can deduce from many of her remarks made in moments of stress, to the sentimental literature and drama of the day. Her simple desire to jump overboard and die in her lover's arms has a distinct literary flavor. The tender revelation of impending motherhood had always worked successfully in books and on the stage. Certainly her wavering lover would not fail to respond to the appealing prospect of tiny garments and the faintly audible patter of little feet.

Considering their intimate relations it might appear surprising that he had not suspected her condition before this, but Nan knew Caesar and she may have believed that he was an unobservant man. At any rate, he was regrettably unmoved by the prospect of fatherhood, and with an unfeeling disregard for literary precedent suggested bluntly that she have an abortion performed.

Nan knew better than to argue with him. "I don't know whether I will get rid of this encumbrance here or wait till I get to London," she said. "What do you think?"

"If you have an operation here it will detain you and you won't be able to get away next Wednesday. They have just as good doctors in London as in New York."

"Yes, I have a friend over there who will help me," Nan replied. "I'll have it done in London."

"Good," said Young. "Barney will furnish you with all the money you need. If you want to communicate with me, do it through Barney and he will see that I get your letters."

Nan denied that she had ever told Young that she was pregnant. With the delicacy that was more prevalent in court a half century ago than it is today, her counsel, Mr. Levy, questioned her in this fashion:

Q. Your figure was good? I mean to say it had not been changed by any process of nature?
A. No.
Q. Miss Patterson, were you ever with child?
A. I beg pardon.
Q. Did you hear the question?
A. I do not understand you.
Q. Don't you know what I mean when I ask you were you ever with child?
A. I understand you now.

Nan finally got the point, and we can fancy her blushing modestly as she replied that she had never been with child—never, that is, except for a slight pregnancy during her marriage to Martin. What happened on that occasion was not explained.

That was Nan's testimony about her alleged pregnancy. Let us return now to McKean's account of the conversation in Reisenweber's:

Q. Did she say anything else about going away?
A. She put her arms around his neck and said, "Caesar, I love you more than Mrs. Young. Why don't you send her away and not send me?"
Q. What did he say to that?
A. He said he could not do it. He could not possibly do it.

Q. What else did he say about it? What expression did he use?
A. I don't remember the expression.
Q. Do you remember a familiar expression of his?
A. "Tut, tut, Nan. Chuck it."
Q. Did he say that to her?
A. Yes, sir. He said, "You know we must part."

Young left them at Reisenweber's to go to the race track and the gallant Mr. McKean invited Nan to lunch. They went up to Pabst's on 125th Street, off the beaten path, where there was less likelihood that a respectable married man would be recognized dining with a chorus girl.

Q. Did you have luncheon there?
A. Yes, sir.
Q. Did the defendant eat anything or only you?
A. I only ate. She would not eat. She said that she could not eat anything at all, that her condition would not permit it.
Q. Did you have any conversation with the defendant there at that café on 125th Street?
A. Yes, sir.
Q. What was it?
A. She said she did not want to go away and leave Frank as she called him. That if he would only put her in a room where she could see him passing every day she would be perfectly satisfied if she could only see him.

Nan's modest desire just to be able to see her lover passing by each day is further indication that she was a girl who read books.

McKean engaged passage for Nan on the *Teutonic* but she did not sail for London. The reason was not explained, but it seems likely that she just refused to go. Young continued to visit her at the Imperial and, according to Mrs. Young, to spend every night with his wife at the Walcott.

CHAPTER SEVEN

The Youngs Plan a Vacation

THE END OF MAY was approaching and the races were about to open at Gravesend. To be near the track Young and his wife took rooms at the Menair Cottage at Sheepshead Bay, and the faithful Millin also took a room at the same place. The Morgan Smiths had moved from their apartment on Sixty-first Street to the St. Paul Hotel at Sixtieth Street and Columbus Avenue, so Nan checked out of the Imperial and moved into a room adjoining her sister's at the same hotel.

Millin later testified that after Young went down to the Menair Cottage he never left Sheepshead Bay, but it is evident that he continued to communicate with Nan and that his wife knew it. There was a temporary calm but the battle was still on and Mrs. Young was gamely fighting to rescue her husband from the snares of the siren.

For some time she had been urging him to take a summer

vacation with her abroad; perhaps if he were a safe distance away from Nan's allurements for two or three months, the infatuation might fade. At last, the day after they arrived at Sheepshead, Young consented to make the trip. Since Nan stubbornly refused to leave him, his only other course was to go away from her.

Mrs. Young was a woman of action and she was not going to give Caesar time to change his mind. That same day she went to New York and booked passage on the *Germanic* to sail at 9:30 on the morning of June fourth.

"What accommodations did you have?" Rand asked her when later she testified in court.

"I believe they were the best on the boat," Mrs. Young answered.

"Will you tell me what you paid for them?"

"Three hundred and fifty dollars—return tickets."

Ah, sad memories of a vanished day! We know that Caesar Young was a reckless spender, and we can be sure that he did not begrudge the three hundred and fifty dollars his wife had squandered for a round trip for two. The best was none too good.

Besides, we know that Young was affluent at that time, despite an unsuccessful effort by the defense to show that he was in financial straits.

"Just before his death," Levy asked Millin, "Caesar Young had lost heavily at the track, hadn't he?"

"No more than usual," Millin replied.

"What do you call usual losses?"

"Oh, he would stand to lose eight or ten thousand dollars in one day."

Certainly nothing to cast a cloud across a jolly vacation abroad!

On the evening of June second Young wrote a letter to one of his stable boys in California and gave it to Millin to mail. Millin neglected to post it and two days later Young was dead so the letter survived to go in evidence at the trial. It is the sort of letter one might expect a horse owner to write to one of his employees—filled with instructions and solicitude for his horses. "Hope you are giving the horses some kind of exercise soon," he wrote, "you know it will take such a long time to get them ready for the fall . . . the St. Carlo colt and Watercure ought to be galloped as soon as possible . . . give Laura another dose of oil . . . and I would keep giving her about 4 quarts of grain each day . . . am enclosing $100 keep tabs how you get rid of it, still expect to hear from you soon. Yours truly, Caesar Young."

June 3, 1904, Caesar Young's last full day on earth, was a busy one for him. There was also activity elsewhere. Sometime on that day a man and a woman entered the pawnshop of Hyman Stern at 516 Sixth Avenue in New York and bought a thirty-two-caliber revolver for which the man paid ten dollars. But more of that anon.

Young arose on the morning of June third at about seven o'clock, and after breakfasting with Millin went with him to the track. At twelve o'clock they returned to Sheepshead Bay, where he had lunch with his wife, and then they went back to the track in time for the first race. "We went to the track in the afternoon," Mrs. Young testified. "Got there about two o'clock and I saw him for a few moments. Didn't see him again—to speak with—until after the fourth race."

Young was not making book that day. The reason his wife did not see him again "to speak with" was that Caesar Young spent the afternoon sitting conspicuously in the grandstand with Nan Patterson and her sister Julia Smith.

There is something about the brazenness and callousness of the man that excites admiration. The decision to go abroad had been a sudden one, and it is not surprising that he should have wanted to tell Nan about it. But it is strange that he should have chosen to break the news in the place where he was better known than anywhere else in the world, and that he should have flaunted his mistress in the presence of the wife with whom he was to leave on the following morning for a second honeymoon.

Nan and the Morgan Smiths had left the St. Paul Hotel early that morning to go to the track, and there is little doubt that Caesar and Nan had met there by appointment. His determination to go abroad had been sudden and this was his delicate way of breaking the news. All of their conversation that afternoon is not recorded but a significant part of it is preserved in Nan's testimony.

Q. Did he say anything when he told you he was going to Europe?

A. Yes. He said he was going to send for me.

Q. Did he say how long he would be away?

A. Not at that conversation. He said I was not to think it was a joke. He was really going. He said he wanted to see me that night, and for me to stay in my room and he would call me up. He said he did not know what time he could get away.

"He said I was not to think it was a joke . . ." Nan was skeptical. It was hard for her to believe that after a year and a half he was actually going away, but Caesar made it bluntly clear that this time it was the real thing. Nan was far too shrewd to believe that once he was in Europe he would send for her. She was fighting desperately but she must have sensed that her rival, sitting alone and humiliated, was winning, and that on the morrow, when the *Germanic* steamed out into the Hudson River, the battle would be over.

After the fourth race Nan and Julia left the grandstand and went down to join Morgan Smith, who was betting busily. When Millin, who had been watching them, saw that they had left, he walked over in front of the judge's stand where he had agreed to meet Young, and together they returned to Mrs. Young.

They waited until the fifth race had been run, and then took the 5:08 train to Long Island City, the ferry across to Thirty-fourth Street, and then a hansom cab to the home of Mrs. Young's sister, Mrs. Luce, where they were going to spend the night before sailing.

Nan and the Smiths waited until the last race had been run and then caught the last train back. As they arrived in New York at about a quarter past six, they were delayed by a crowd that was gathered in front of the ferry house. There had been an accident of some sort and an ambulance was standing nearby, a fact that was later verified at the trial. This episode is important in establishing the time of their arrival, for there was some evidence later that at six o'clock that afternoon a man and a woman had gone into Hyman Stern's pawnshop to buy a revolver. Nan and the Smiths pushed their way through the crowd and took a streetcar uptown to the St. Paul Hotel.

At the Luces' on 140th Street there was a farewell party for the Youngs, and the family and some friends were there. Besides the Luces there were the McKeans, a friend of Mrs. Young—Mrs. Collin—a Mr. and Mrs. Fleischer, and Millin and his sister. This was more than a mere farewell celebration. Every person there knew of Young's entanglement with Nan, and there was a feeling of relief that only a few hours remained before his liberation.

Meanwhile Nan and the Smiths went over to Healy's Restaurant at Sixty-sixth Street and Columbus Avenue for dinner. Before leaving the St. Paul Hotel Nan told the telephone operator that she was expecting a message. "If Mr. Young calls tell him I have gone to Healy's to dine. If anyone else calls, simply say I'm out."

When they returned to the hotel the operator said, "Mr. Young called while you were out and said that he would call you up at Healy's." Nan returned to the restaurant, accompanied by her brother-in-law, Morgan Smith. Nan's morals may not have been beyond reproach, but in the year 1904 it would never have done for her to enter a restaurant at night without a male escort. At Healy's they gave her the message that Young had left for her. She was to remain at the St. Paul and be ready to meet him when he called again, no matter how late it was.

"I returned to the hotel a second time," Nan testified, "and I stayed there until about eleven o'clock when he telephoned me to take an elevated train and meet him at 140th Street. I got a bellboy to take me to the station." Nan was ever a stickler for the proprieties.

At the Luces' the party continued pleasantly. The ladies stayed indoors and gossiped and assisted Mrs. Young in putting the last-minute touches to her packing. Since it was a balmy June night the men sat outdoors on the stoop. From time to time they would stroll down to Pepper's saloon at the corner of 140th Street and Eighth Avenue and have a few drinks. According to Luce, Young made about a dozen such trips, and on one of the visits to Pepper's he went to a telephone and called Nan.

CHAPTER EIGHT

Nan and Caesar Stay Up Late

AT ELEVEN O'CLOCK Young and Luce paid another visit to Pepper's, and Young had several more drinks. Luce took a cigar. He always took a cigar, and he must have accumulated quite a collection that night. Then they went outside and stood on the corner for a while and presently Nan descended the "El" stairs.

"Young was waiting with another man," she testified, "and I started to walk by, but he whistled to me and I walked back to him."

"What did he whistle?" Levy asked.

"His regular whistle when he wanted to attract my attention—'Tell Me, Pretty Maiden.' "

Caesar introduced her to Luce and told his brother-in-law to meet them at one o'clock at McKeever's saloon at 125th Street and Eighth Avenue. Young hailed a cab and drove off with Nan, unmindful that a farewell party in his honor was in progress. Luce, remembering his duties as a host, returned home, where he remained until it was time to leave for McKeever's saloon.

"We drove through Central Park for about an hour," Nan testified.

> Q. What did you talk about while in the cab?
>
> A. He said that he had to go away. He asked me how much money I had and I told him not more than four or five hundred dollars. He gave me a hundred dollars more and told me that would help to meet some expenses while he was on the trip. I didn't give him any definite answer. We talked about England and he told me about a chum he had over there. We went back to 125th Street and into a restaurant where Mr. Luce was waiting for us. He did not come to our table. Mr. Young told me he wanted to talk to me alone, and that I must not say anything to Mr. Luce about following him to England.

On cross-examination Nan said that the hundred dollars was in twenty-dollar bills. She put them in her stocking because there was no room in her handbag. Five twenty-dollar bills are not very bulky, but Nan was a careful girl and handbags are easily lost.

At one o'clock in the morning, as Mrs. Young sat up waiting for the return of her errant husband, Caesar and Nan arrived at McKeever's saloon. Luce obediently was already there in front of the door, so instead of going inside they walked over to Flannery's saloon at 125th Street and St. Nicholas Avenue, went into a back room and sat down.

The room was L-shaped and Luce did not join them but sat down around the corner about four or five feet away. "I could see them anytime I looked by craning a little," he testified.

We might pause here for a moment to consider one of the many puzzles in this case. Why did Caesar Young ask Luce to come along that night? If for any reason he wanted a witness to his conversation with Nan, why did he drive around Central Park alone with her for an hour before meeting Luce? And why, if he wanted a witness, did he have Luce sit around a corner where he could see them only by craning, and where he could hear them only if they spoke in loud voices? And why did he want a witness at all?

They had arrived at Flannery's around one o'clock in the morning and remained until almost three, Young drinking all the while. Luce thought that he drank beer or ale, which was corroborated by the bartender, but Nan insisted that Young had "fifteen or twenty drinks of whisky straight." This, in addition to the drinks consumed during the numerous visits to Pepper's at 140th Street, accounts for a considerable amount of liquor that night. Each time they had a drink Luce took a cigar.

Nan and Caesar "were quarreling," Luce said, "and having angry words with one another." Nan was crying, but Luce did not hear much of what was said because, he explained, "I did not pay much attention."

From one to three is a long time, and a lot of conversation can take place in two hours, so Luce may be forgiven if he couldn't remember all of it. However, he did conveniently manage to pay close attention during a dramatic moment in the quarrel and professed to remember it later with verbatim accuracy. This fragment became an important link in the prosecution's case against Nan.

"You are not going!" she cried.

"Damn it," Young answered angrily, "you don't know what boat I am going on!"

"Oh, yes," Nan answered, "I do know what boat you are going on."

"I'll bet you a hundred dollars to fifty cents you cannot name the boat I am going on," Young said.

At that he took a large roll of bills from his pocket, peeled off a hundred-dollar bill, and tossed it to Luce.

"There, Bill," Young exclaimed. "Damn it, if she can name the boat, I am going to give her that hundred-dollar bill!"

"I could name the boat," Nan replied, "but I wouldn't give you the satisfaction of telling you what boat you are going on. Don't think you will get up early in the morning and get down there and get on the boat and go down in the hold where I can't find you. I will be there and I will find you all right, and you won't go!"

Were these words, spoken in anger a few hours before Young's death, the murder threat? Mr. Rand contended that they were, and he used them powerfully at the trial. It must be borne in mind, however, that we have only Luce's word for it that they were spoken, and that Luce, like the other brother-in-law, McKean, was a biased witness.

Nan, who also was a strongly interested witness, denied that she had ever said anything of the sort. Her version of the conversation, at least the part to which Luce did not pay attention, was that Young spoke of his reluctance to leave her and his plan to send for her after he arrived in Europe.

At about a quarter of three Caesar and Nan went over to Luce's table and they all left the saloon together. Young was "profane and angry" and he directed Luce to call a hansom.

"Now we will all go down together," Young said.

"No, we won't," Nan replied.

"God damn it," Young said, "then you will go home alone!"

Luce called another cab and Young grabbed Nan by the arm and forced her roughly into it.

"He pushed her against the hansom," Crowley, the cab driver, testified. "When she refused to get in he slapped her face and told her to get in or he would knock her goddamned head off." She sobbed all the way to her hotel, the cab driver said.

Crowley was certainly an impartial witness, so it should be noted that Nan's version of what occurred differs somewhat from his. On direct examination she gave this testimony:

Q. Did you quarrel at parting?

A. We did not. He wanted me to ride up to 140th Street and then go back to the hotel but I would not. That made him angry but he put me in a cab and kissed me good night.

Q. Did he strike you?

A. No. He pushed me with his hands, but it was a habit of his when he was drinking. It was just fun and it did not hurt me.

Q. When you left him that night did you expect to see him the next morning?

A. I did not.

Q. Were you sobbing on the drive to the hotel?

A. I do not think so. I reached the hotel and went right to bed. I was tired out.

Later, under cross-examination by Mr. Rand she modified the story.

Q. When you left Young that night, did you have any intention of following him on to Europe?

A. I did not.

Q. Did he suppose that you would?

A. Yes.

Q. Did you feel bad about deceiving him?

A. Yes, but I didn't show signs of grieving by crying.

Q. You loved him and it must have occurred to you that he was going away with his wife. Didn't you care at all?

A. Yes, I cared and now I remember that I cried.

Q. When Mr. Levy questioned you you said you could not think of any reason you could have had for crying that night. Why have you changed since yesterday?

A. I was nervous yesterday. Now I am getting used to being questioned. Today I remember.

Q. As a matter of fact, then, you are less nervous when I question you than when Mr. Levy questions you.

A. I am used to being up here now.

Young and Luce arrived at 140th Street at a quarter of four; they got out of the cab at the corner and walked to the house. Perhaps they thought they could slip into the house unnoticed, but Mrs. Young and Mrs. Luce were waiting up for them.

"Do you doubt," Rand declared to the jury in his summing up, "that when Young went to his sleep that night he was a man marked for slaughter?"

CHAPTER NINE

Nan and Caesar Go for a Drive

ON SATURDAY, June 4, 1904, the *Germanic* was to sail at 9:30 A.M., and Caesar Young, despite his big night the night before, arose early. Luce met him as he was leaving the house at about a quarter past seven. He said that he was "going out to buy a new hat and get a shave and then going down to the boat." It is not reported whether he had any breakfast that morning; Mr. Levy tried to convince the jury that Young had had several drinks on an empty stomach. However that may be, it was evident that he had been drinking when he met Nan about an hour later.

Nan, who had arrived home about four in the morning, also awoke early, but not intentionally. The telephone rang between seven and eight and Julia Smith answered it.* It was Young, who said he wanted to speak to Nan.

* We have, of course, only Julia Smith's word for what took

"She's asleep," her sister told him.

"Well, try to rouse her," Young said. When he telephoned again a few minutes later, Nan had been awakened and was dressing. "Tell her to meet me right away at Columbus Circle," he told Julia Smith, who again answered the telephone. He must have been quite impatient for, according to Mrs. Smith, he telephoned three times while Nan was dressing. "Tell her to hurry," he said.

"She is hurrying," her sister replied. "She's on her way now."

At length she was ready, and as she left the hotel room, attractively dressed in a violet walking suit and carrying a pair of white kid gloves in her hand, her sister came hurrying after her down the hallway. Nan had forgotten her black handbag. The bag had been left open on the bureau and as Mrs. Smith handed it to her she had the prophetic foresight to look into it and observe that it contained only a handkerchief. Certainly anything as bulky as a thirty-two-caliber revolver would not have escaped Julia Smith's sisterly eye.

Nan hurried to Columbus Circle, and, as she told it on the witness stand, "Shortly before eight o'clock I went to Fifty-ninth Street. Mr. Young was there. He began cursing and asked me why I did not come sooner. I knew he was drinking because he had his hair pulled down over one eye as he always did when he was under the influence of liquor.

"We went into a saloon by the rear entrance and he ordered a drink of brandy and of whisky. He drank them both. We

---

place that morning before Nan left the Hotel Navarre. Julia was a strongly partisan witness and her testimony in court must be considered with caution.

walked to the Circle and had two more drinks. Then we got into a cab and I heard him tell the driver to stop at a hat store. We drove to a hat store and he got out and bought a new hat."

Nan's direct examination continued:

Q. Did he say where he was taking you?

A. No. If I had any idea he was going to the pier, I would not have gone. When we got back into the cab after buying the hat, the cab kept on downtown, and we got out and he bought two more drinks in a saloon in some street under the elevated railroad.

Nan knew that the steamer was leaving at 9:30. One wonders where on earth she thought they were going.

The saloon was on the corner of Bleecker Street and West Broadway, and we will let Frederick Wollins, the bartender, tell what happened there:

Q. What was the condition of the two people? Were they sober?

A. Sober.

Levy's comment was "To a bartender all customers are sober."

Q. Was there any quarrel of any kind there between them?

A. No, sir.

Q. What did they order?

A. Two whiskies.

Q. How much were the drinks?

A. Twenty cents.

We can be sure that Young, always extravagant, ordered the very best brand. While they were in the saloon, he took from his pocket a picture postcard on which there was a picture of Tappan's Restaurant at Sheepshead Bay and wrote Nan's name and address on it and handed it to her. She put it in her handbag, where it was found after her arrest. Nan did not explain the card and it puzzled the lawyers at the trial. One of the theories suggested by the defense was that Young might have intended to shoot her and that he wanted her to have some identification upon her. This seems like a rather wild hypothesis. The prosecution suggested that he meant to mail it from the ship, but why a picture of Tappan's? And why give it to her if he intended to mail it?

We may speculate at this point whether, if there was a pistol in her bag, she would have risked exposing it to Young when she opened her bag to put the card in.

After they came out of the saloon they got back into the cab. Nan's direct testimony continued:

"He began talking again as he had been about my coming to England after him. I told him that I really did not want to go; that after things had quieted down and Mrs. Young had forgotten me I might feel differently. 'Do you really mean that?' he asked me. 'I have lost a lot of money and now I am going to lose my girl.' I then heard a muffled sound and he fell forward in my lap! I saw no pistol. He half raised himself again and I began to scold him, not realizing what happened. Then he fell forward and I could not attract his attention. It seemed hours before I could get anyone to help me. Finally a policeman got on the front of the cab and I was so glad that I cannot express it."

In reply to her lawyer's question Nan emphatically swore that she did not shoot Caesar Young.

"That is all," her lawyer said, and the court adjourned.

On the following day Mr. Rand cross-examined the defendant at great length.

Q. You said yesterday that you had no thought of where you were going when you got in the cab on the morning of June fourth. Didn't you know that he was going away for two months, and that the vessel on which he was to sail left that morning?

A. I had no idea where we were going. That is all. I had an idea that we might be going somewhere near where the boat was leaving from.

Q. When did you first tell Young that you were not going to follow him to Europe?

A. In the last saloon we stopped at I told him I didn't fancy it. It was when we had gotten back in the cab that I told him that there was no use in my pretending that I was going because I was not. He seemed very much surprised.

Q. What did he do then?

A. He got my hand and pulled me toward him with so much force that it hurt.

Q. Did he kiss you?

A. No.

Q. He pulled you toward him twice, didn't he?

A. Yes. I wrenched myself loose and he grabbed me again.

Q. Was it when he seized you the first time that he said he was going to lose his girl?

A. It was between pulls.

Q. What did you do then?

A. When I freed myself a second time I looked out of the window. I didn't want him to see how much he had hurt me. The pain was so severe that the tears came to my eyes.

Q. And you turned away to hide your tears when you heard the shot?

A. It was all so quick that I am not positive.

Q. Where were you looking when the shot came?

A. I was looking away from him to the left.

Q. Did you see a pistol?

A. I didn't. I was not looking that way at all.

Q. Will you describe the sound of the shot you heard?

A. It was a muffled sound—smothered.

Q. You are certain about that?

A. Yes. At first I thought it came from the street. Then I saw the smoke.

Michaels, the cab driver, described the sound as a "loud report" but he was neither disturbed nor curious to find out what caused it as he continued on his unhurried way. But immediately after the pistol shot Nan pushed up the trap door in the roof of the cab. "The lady raised the trap," Michaels said, "and told me to drive to a drugstore."

"Didn't she say, 'For God's sake drive to a drugstore!" Levy asked him on cross-examination.

"That I couldn't swear to," Michaels replied. "I don't remember."

They stopped at a nearby drugstore and Nan, almost hysterical, cried, "Hurry! Call that man out!" and Michaels summoned the proprietor out onto the sidewalk and told him that a man had been shot in his cab. The druggist directed him to the nearby Hudson Street Hospital.

A young man named William Stemm was standing on the sidewalk with his back to the street. As he heard what he described as "the sound of a shot," he turned around and saw smoke coming out of the cab. Being naturally curious, he followed the cab to the drugstore. He was positive, he testified, that the doors of the cab were open, but as it drove away the driver closed them. Stemm climbed on the back step and drove along to the hospital.

As they left the drugstore a police officer, Patrolman William J. Junior, who was directing traffic at the intersection of Franklin Street and West Broadway, stopped the cab and jumped on the step.

The doors of the cab were now closed and as the driver swung them open Junior looked inside. Nan was seated on the left side of the cab, and Young, who had been sitting at her right, was toppled over. His head lay in her lap, his right arm dangled between her knees, and his left arm was around her waist. His hat was on the floor of the cab. Nan's white gloves lay neatly folded upon her knees beside the head of her prostrate companion.

Officer Junior asked Nan what had happened and she replied that the man had shot himself. At that he directed Michaels to hurry to the hospital. During the five-minute drive, Junior testified, Nan was sobbing and wringing her hands and exclaiming over and over again, "Oh Caesar, Caesar, what have you done!"

In spite of her distraught condition, Junior, who was an alert officer, managed to question her. The man, she told him, was Caesar Young, the bookmaker. Junior asked her what had happened to the pistol and she replied, "I don't know." Thereupon he looked around the cab and examined the lifeless body. Young was wearing a sack coat, and in the right-hand pocket Junior found the gun, still warm.

"How did it happen?" Junior asked her.

"He told me he was going away," Nan answered, "might be away for three months, might not see me for three months, or he may never see me, and as he said that he shot himself."

We might point out here that Nan's statements in the cab, made under great emotional stress, do not differ essentially from the story she later told in court. Did her anguished cry, "Oh Caesar, Caesar, what have you done!" indicate, as Mr. Rand contended, extraordinary presence of mind, or was it, as Mr. Levy argued, a spontaneous outpouring of agonized grief?

When the cab arrived at the hospital Young was dead. Nan followed the body into the operating room, and as it was placed upon the operating table she threw herself upon the corpse of her lover, embracing it and sobbing hysterically. With difficulty Officer Junior pulled her away and led her into an adjoining room, where she fainted.

Young Stemm, who was determined not to miss anything, was also present in the operating room. He testified that Nan was crying and exclaiming, "Look at me, Frank! Why did you do it?"

At the hospital Officer Junior turned Nan over to Detective Edward J. Quinn, who took her in Michael's cab to the Leonard Street police station. As yet she was not accused of anything, but she was being detained as a material witness. Nan carried her white gloves and her bag, the handle of which was broken. "It was broken in the excitement," she explained. On the way to the station house Quinn questioned her. By this time she had somewhat recovered her composure.

"Why did this man shoot himself?" Quinn asked her.

"Are you an officer?" she inquired, and Quinn replied that he was.

Then Nan said, "I may as well tell you as I will have to tell it anyway. You know, Caesar Young and I have been lovers for the past two and a half years. He is a married man and his wife was causing an awful lot of trouble. He said he was going away and I might not see him again for three months, and I might never see him."

When they got to the station house Nan again fainted. After she was revived Quinn took her in to Captain Sweeney, the officer in charge of the precinct. "I am going to ask you some questions," Captain Sweeney said, "and you can answer them if you like, or you may not."

"I will answer any questions," she replied.

This was not more than two hours after the shooting and we might consider, at this point, whether this was the conduct of a woman who had just committed a deliberate murder, or one who felt secure in the consciousness of innocence. Captain Sweeney asked her about the events leading up to the shooting, the events of the night before, of meeting Young at Columbus Circle, and what took place in the cab driving downtown. There are some minor discrepancies between the version she gave Sweeney and her testimony on the stand, but, on the whole, the story was substantially the same. There was, however, one important additional fact. It will be remembered that in the cab Nan had told Officer Junior that she didn't know where the pistol was. This, according to Captain Sweeney, is what she told him:

". . . she said she heard a muffled sound, and as she turned around Mr. Young fell over onto her lap. She said she felt around the back of the seat to see what had caused the sound, whether it was a pistol or where did the pistol go. She said she put her hand into his pocket and felt the butt end of a revolver, and as soon as she did she dropped it, because if there was anything in her life she was afraid of, it was a pistol."

On cross-examination Captain Sweeney was asked:

Q. Now, Captain, during the whole of this conversation with her, did she answer the questions freely?
A. She did.
Q. Without hesitation?
A. Yes, sir.
Q. Upon the instant of your putting a question she immediately answered?
A. Why, I should say she did.

When Young did not arrive, his wife and friends, waiting nervously at the pier, feared that he might have met with an accident. Just before the gangplank was pulled up, the Youngs' luggage was removed from the ship, and at 9:30 as the *Germanic* pulled out into the river, Mrs. Young remained behind on the pier with her friends.

They waited there, worried, for some time, and then Luce telephoned to a newspaper office to try to get some information about his missing brother-in-law and was told of the shooting. Already the extras were rolling off the presses. It was agreed not to tell Mrs. Young at that time—she didn't learn of her husband's death until half past three in the afternoon—and after she had left the pier with her sisters Millin jumped into a cab and dashed across town to the police station.

He arrived while Nan was giving her statement to Captain Sweeney. He tried to force his way into Sweeney's office, and as he was held back by the police he cried, "I could kill that woman! She cannot deceive me. I knew Young since we were boys together!"

He turned to one of the reporters and said, "She would not dare to come out of that room if she knew I was here. She knows that I know that she attempted to destroy the happiness of the Young family. She knows that I know that Caesar Young did not take his own life. Why, that woman's career has been one of destruction. Young did not commit suicide. He is the third to die on her account!"*

As he spoke, the door of Sweeney's office opened and Nan came out. When she saw Millin she became deathly pale and shrank back. In terror she put her hands up to her eyes and tried to hide behind Captain Sweeney, who stood in the doorway. "If I had a gun I'd kill you!" Millin shouted. "What did you do to Caesar?"

From the station house Nan was taken to the coroner's office, where she was arraigned before Coroner Brown. As she stood there waiting for her case to be called, she saw a billy sticking out of Detective Quinn's pocket. "I wish you would hit me over the head with that thing you have in your pocket." Detective Quinn asked her why. "To kill me," she replied.

* Millin may have had in mind the stories that had been current about the death of Fred Herr. Who the third person was I have no idea.

Meanwhile the Morgan Smiths had been notified of her arrest and had hurried down to court. Smith realized that Nan had to have a lawyer, so he got in touch with the firm of Levy and Unger in the World Building, the leading criminal lawyers in the city. They quickly dispatched one of their attorneys to the coroner's court.

At first Coroner Brown was inclined to release Nan on $5,000 bail, but as he was discussing it the report of the autopsy arrived, which altered the situation. There were too many suspicious circumstances to risk turning her loose, and she was committed to the Tombs.

As the iron bars of the jail loomed up before her, she collapsed and had to be carried inside, where she was placed in a hospital cell. She had had a busy day.

CHAPTER TEN

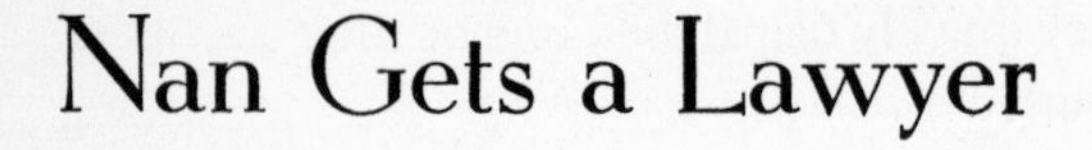

Nan Gets a Lawyer

THAT NIGHT BANNER HEADLINES were spread across the front pages of the newspapers.

"CAESAR" YOUNG, RICH BOOKMAKER, SHOT AND KILLED
WHILE IN A CAB WITH FLORADORA SWEETHEART

This was the headline that filled half of the first page of the *Evening Journal.*

All the newspapers printed pictures of Nan in her *Floradora* costume, and there was rejoicing in Park Row. For about a year and a half the case of Nan Patterson was the outstanding news of the day.

There were few criminal cases of importance in New York during the early years of the century in which the law firm of Levy and Unger did not play a part. Their offices were in the World Building, now, sadly, torn down, an imposing sky-scraper more than fifteen stories high that looked out over the roofs of the city and the low-lying skyline of Brooklyn.

Henry W. Unger was what is sometimes called a "lawyer's lawyer." He had been an assistant district attorney for many years, having started in the prosecutor's offices as stenographer to the Grand Jury, and rising to become the head of the Indictment Bureau.

There was no lawyer in the city who knew his way among the intricate mazes of criminal law as well as he did. He was essentially a student, and although he made many courtroom appearances, his greatest happiness was in the library poring over the lawbooks and writing briefs that were models of learning and clarity. Many of the ingenious points of law that made Levy and Unger so valuable to their clients and so feared by their opponents in the district attorney's office originated in Unger's resourceful brain.

In 1900 he resigned from the district attorney's office to form a partnership with his old friend Abraham Levy, who was then at the height of his fame as the outstanding criminal advocate in New York. The following year Unger ran for district attorney against William Travers Jerome and was defeated. Four years later the political adversaries were to face each other in the courtroom as prosecution and defense counsel.

In 1904, the year of the Nan Patterson case, Abraham Levy (or Abe Levy, as the newspapers used to call him) was forty-three years old and at the peak of his powers. Arthur Train, who was a brilliant prosecutor as well as a splendid author, once told me that he considered Abe Levy the greatest criminal lawyer that this country had ever produced. In speaking of his celebrated fictional character, Mr. Tutt, Train said, "I compounded him out of three characters—Abe Levy, Abraham Lincoln, and Jesus Christ." Years later, Alexander Woollcott, who had covered the criminal courts for the New York *Times* in his younger days, described him as "the mighty Abe Levy . . . the most adroit and zestful practitioner of the criminal law in this country."

He had been born in London, and although he was only six years old when he came to this country, he always retained a charming trace of an English accent. He had a beautifully mellow voice and a virtuoso command of the English language; and in an age when oratory was a fine art he had few peers.

It was my rare privilege to assist him in many cases. Like most successful jury lawyers he was a consummate actor and could play upon the emotions of his listeners as a musician plays upon an instrument, ranging from satire to indignation and pathos, and shedding real tears when the occasion required it.

He had a delightful sense of humor and a ready wit that endeared him to juries and always made one of his trials not only an exhibition of legal artistry but rare entertainment. Whenever he tried a case the courtroom was filled with spectators, young lawyers, and reporters, for, whatever the nature of the case, he always put on a good show. It was his popularity with the newspapermen, I believe, that was largely responsible for the good press that Nan Patterson got.

One of his outstanding professional attributes was a suavity of manner and unfailing courtesy to the court. Many judges have told me that he was the most gracious lawyer who ever appeared before them, but beneath his courteous manner was the dynamic force of a powerful personality. He was a mighty cross-examiner.

He had few clients of his own; he was the equivalent of an

English barrister, and in most of his cases he was retained by other lawyers. At the time of his death in 1920 he had tried more than three hundred homicide cases, an all-time record, I believe, as well as countless cases of other kinds.

These were the lawyers who were retained to defend Nan Patterson. The partners were as unlike in appearance as they were in talents and temperament. Unger was a slim, mild-mannered man whose gentleness was deceptively concealed behind a bushy black beard. Levy was almost entirely bald, short, stout and clean-shaven—the image, as many people used to say, of Mr. Pickwick.

The firm of Levy and Unger was a great team, and, although Nan Patterson may not have known it as she lay upon her prison cot that first night in the Tombs, she could not have been in more competent hands.

The first move Nan's lawyers made was to seek out a writ of habeas corpus in the Supreme Court to have her released on bail. She was brought into court by the sheriff, clad in deep black. After an extended legal argument, Justice John Proctor Clarke concluded that there was reason to believe that a homicide had been committed; the writ was dismissed, and Nan went back to the Tombs.

Meanwhile the district attorney's office was busily preparing the case for presentation to the Grand Jury. The job was entrusted to an able young assistant, Francis Garvan, who later became prominent as an industrialist. Mr. Garvan interviewed every witness who conceivably might have been able to throw some light upon the case. Among them was J. Morgan Smith, the husband of Nan's sister Julia.

Smith was a tall, florid man—the sort that is sometimes described as the sporting type. He claimed to be related in some way to J. P. Morgan, but as Smith's name began to figure prominently in the press, a statement was released from the austere offices at Wall and Broad that Mr. Morgan had never heard of him.

Nevertheless, Smith did come from a wealthy family and after being compelled to leave school for "certain irregularities"—one story said the school was Princeton—he came to New York and actually did work for the Morgan firm at five dollars a week. He lived at that time in a boardinghouse at 137 West 47th Street and his income was augmented by an allowance he received from his mother.

Then he went to Europe and traveled extensively, returning to New York in 1897. In 1899 he appeared in San Francisco with a wild yarn of having been shanghaied aboard a whaling vessel from which he deserted in the Far North. He told many lurid stories of his adventures—of having been shipwrecked and of fighting the natives in the Philippines.

It seems apparent that Morgan Smith was a man with a fertile imagination and not too high a regard for truth. He claimed to be in the insurance business, but if he was, his insurance business was carried on for the most part at race tracks and expensive barrooms. About a year before the shooting, he married Nan's sister Julia, who had been a clerk in the auditor's office of the War Department. Mr. Rand tried to make it appear that the Smiths had been living off the bounty of Caesar Young. There was no proof of this, but it seems quite possible.

Since Smith plays an important role in this story, I would like to quote a description of him that appeared in the New York *Evening Journal:*

> He is a full six feet tall and bulky in proportion though not ungainly. His manner is careless and rather boyish. His reddish hair is thin and there is a perceptible bald spot, although he is little more than thirty years old. His face is smooth shaven and of the pinkish coloring known as a sandy complexion. He has a barely noticeable nervous twitching of the muscles of his face and a very slight impediment in his speech. Altogether he is rather colorless. He defers to his wife and seems to rely greatly upon her judgment.

On June seventh, three days after the shooting, Smith was called down to Assistant District Attorney Garvan's office and questioned. He refused to answer any questions on the ground that the answers might tend to incriminate or degrade him. He stated that he had nothing to conceal or fear, but since his sister-in-law was facing an accusation of murder, he felt that out of loyalty to her he should rely upon his constitutional rights. That night he was served with a subpoena to appear before the Grand Jury that was about to begin its inquiry into the case.

Meanwhile the police were combing the city and the adjacent regions in an effort to trace the revolver that had fired the fatal shot. The Grand Jury hearings commenced on June ninth, and that night the newspapers announced that an unnamed pawnbroker had appeared before the Grand Jury.

The following evening, June tenth, a startling story appeared in the *Evening Journal.*

> NAN PATTERSON'S SISTER VANISHES
> SELLER OF PISTOL FOUND
>
> J. Morgan Smith and wife, brother-in-law and sister of "Nan" Patterson have mysteriously disappeared from their apartments at the St. Paul Hotel, and Supreme Court Justice

> Newburger has issued a body attachment for Smith and his wife. They are wanted as witnesses.
>
> A man and a woman purchased the revolver at Hyman Stern's pawnshop, No. 516 Sixth Avenue, less than twenty hours before the tragedy. Nan Patterson was not the woman.

The *Evening World* said:

> The hotel manager could tell nothing about the destination of the Smiths when they left the hotel. An expressman drove up to the hotel yesterday and took away several trunks belonging to them. The detectives tried to trace the baggage, but they could not get a clue.

The story about the pawnbroker in the *Telegram* on June tenth said:

> Mr. Stern was then shown a picture of Caesar Young, an excellent likeness. He took the photograph in his hands and after looking at it carefully shook his head and said that it was not a picture of the purchaser of the revolver.
>
> "That is not the man," he said. "It looks nothing like him. The man who purchased the weapon is of a type entirely different. I judge that this is a picture of a man much smaller than the one who bought the revolver. That man was as heavy as myself and probably ten or fifteen pounds heavier. (Mr. Stern weighs about 200 pounds.) I am five feet eight inches tall, and he was a good bit taller than I. He was about thirty years old. He was well dressed and from his conversation I took him to be a man about town."

The *Telegram* then added this comment: "That description fits J. Morgan Smith precisely."

It will appear later that the testimony the pawnbroker gave on the witness stand was different from the story printed in the *Telegram*. Certainly the reporter could not have been in the Grand Jury room, and of course he did not make it up, so presumably the story was given out by the district attorney's office.

The practice of "trying a case in the newspapers" is a pernicious one and has been condemned in recent years by the bar associations and the canons of professional ethics. It deprives a defendant of a fair trial if statements are broadcast without benefit of oath and the acid test of cross-examination. The practice still unfortunately continues, but there was far greater abuse fifty years ago than there is today.

District Attorney Jerome was a master of the art of publicity and he had no scruples about using it in a criminal case, but, as will appear, his opponents, Levy and Unger, were no amateurs either. If, as has been said, Waterloo was won on the playing fields of Eton, it can be said with equal truth that many murder trials at the beginning of the century were won in the pages of the *World* and the *Journal* as much as in the courtroom.

On June thirteenth Nan Patterson was indicted for murder in the first degree. It was reported that the Grand Jury had hesitated about bringing in a true bill, but their doubts had been resolved by the flight of the Smiths. The following day she was arraigned in Part One of the Court of General Sessions before Judge Newburger to plead to the indictment. She was dressed in deep black and wore a heavy black veil—mourning, presumably, for the late Mr. Young.

When the defendant appeared in court, the story in the *Evening Journal* said:

NAN PATTERSON IS A PHYSICAL WRECK

The Nan Patterson who appeared before Judge Newburger today to plead to an indictment charging her with murder was not the Nan Patterson who got into a hansom cab with Caesar Young a week ago Saturday morning. That was a girl with a fresh, blooming face and bright eyes, a jaunty, self-possessed girl, sure of her looks and her ability to take care of herself.

It was a jaded drooping woman who stood before the bar of Justice and heard her lawyer protest against her indictment in terms, the import of which was not clear. Since her arrest Nan Patterson has aged ten years. Her face is sallow and her eyes are sunken. Her hair hangs in straggling bunches, and her white hands are thin.

Her appetite has left her. She ate nothing this morning before going to court, nor did she eat any dinner last night. The nervous strain to which she has been subjected has led to a physical breakdown. . . .

The New York *World* said:

So far as is known nothing has been heard from J. Morgan Smith by either Nan Patterson or her lawyers, and it is not believed that the District Attorney is making any effort to find him. Should Smith return, the District Attorney runs a chance that he will not be identified by Stern, the pawnbroker, as the man who bought the revolver with which Young was killed.

The case was only ten days old but clearly the *World* and the *Journal* were already on Nan's side.

The pleading to the indictment had been postponed to enable the lawyers to make certain motions, but ten days later Nan again appeared in court and pleaded not guilty. Meanwhile there had been no dearth of news. Nan's venerable father, an impressive old gentleman with long, flowing white dundrearies, had appeared on the scene to rally to his daughter's support, and the papers were filled with heart-rending tales of Nan's old mother who was languishing in Washington, D. C., stricken by the shock of her daughter's plight.

Some unkind commentators suggested that the ancient father and the drooping dundrearies were an artful bit of stagecraft contrived by Nan's resourceful counsel, but this was not true. The father was unquestionably authentic and so was the ailing mother.

The *Evening Journal* on June twenty-second reported the sequel to Nan's appearance in court.

> It was after she left court that the Patterson woman was called upon to bear the greatest shock. Yesterday morning an intimate friend of the Patterson family arrived from Washington to break to the gray-haired father of "Nan" Patterson the news that the physicians in attendance on his sick wife at her home in Washington had decided, after consultation, that her heart was in bad state, and that any shock, however slight, coming at this time, would undoubtedly result fatally.
>
> The duty the loving father had to perform was to break the news to his daughter, already almost crazed by her confinement and the horrible scenes she had been called upon to witness since her incarceration, that her mother was near death's door.
>
> Gently the feeble old man broke the news, and with a shriek the girl fell to her knees, grasping him about the knees, and crying aloud.
>
> Then the girl swooned, and it was some time before the restoratives applied brought her to consciousness again.

The main battle, in the courtroom, still lay ahead, but daily Mr. Levy was clamoring for an early trial so that his delicate client would not have to endure a summer in the Tombs, and it was evident that the defense had scored several points in the preliminary propaganda skirmishes.

CHAPTER ELEVEN

"... Nor Iron Bars a Cage"

MEANWHILE the search for the Smiths went on; "scores" of policemen and detectives had been assigned to find them. They were in Washington, D. C., they were in Virginia, they had gone out West, they were everywhere except the one place where their presence was urgently needed—the Criminal Courts Building in New York.

Each day communiqués were issued from the opposing camps. As Levy continued to plead plaintively for a speedy trial and lament the absence of the missing witnesses, Garvan countered with a statement: "We will be ready to try this case at two o'clock this afternoon if the Smiths are produced."

Levy informed the reporters that he had learned "in a roundabout way" that J. Morgan Smith and his wife were in a sanitarium within fifty miles of New York. "Mr. Smith is simply suffering from nervous prostration," said the lawyer. "He has nothing to fear." It was not explained whether, by a remarkable coincidence, Mrs. Smith was also suffering from nervous prostration, nor what prevented her from picking up a telephone and revealing to an anxious public, including her sister's lawyers, where she and her husband were.

The hunt for the absent Smiths went on and, as the summer approached, Nan continued to languish in the Tombs. Apparently she did not languish very much. Instead of partaking of the Spartan prison fare, she was served with special food sent in from an expensive restaurant, and her cell was filled with gifts of books, fruit and candy sent in by her many admirers.

Strangely enough, Nan did not appreciate fully the comforts of the Tombs. "I cannot see what they have against me to hold me here so long," she confided with girlish wistfulness to a reporter from the *Evening Journal.* "I cannot complain of the treatment here, but when I think of the bright sunshine and the free air of the country where I should be today, it's pretty hard."

Nevertheless the regrettable absence of free air and bright sunshine agreed with her, and she put on weight. Each day she was visited by her venerable father, whose drooping whiskers and loyal devotion aroused the compassion of the tender-hearted reporters.

Letters of sympathy poured in from all over the country, including, her father told the press, two or more offers of marriage each day. Said the New York *World:*

> After calling upon his daughter today in the Tombs Mr. Patterson announced that she had received among the letters in today's mail, two offers of marriage.
>
> "The first offer," said Mr. Patterson, "came from a farmer in Indiana. He wrote that he owned two good farms and that he always had a weakness for theatrical women and that he had fallen in love with my daughter after seeing her picture in a weekly paper. He wound up his letter with: 'I firmly be-

lieve that you are innocent and pray you most earnestly to consider honorably my proposal.'

"The second offer of marriage was from a farmer in Iowa who signed himself Thompson who wrote: 'If you are willing to marry me I will do my best to make you happy. I own a big farm which for the past two years has proved to be very prosperous, and I can offer you a respectable home.

"'I have seen your photograph and judge from that you are strong and good-looking and will make me a good wife, though I don't expect you to do any manual work. I confess there is little amusement here, but you will have plenty of money to spend. And perhaps the opportunity given here for you to live down your past will furnish you sufficient inducement to come. Don't think that I am a crank. I mean what I say. I love you and want you to marry me.'"

These lovelorn gentlemen assumed that Nan would be speedily freed and so did a large part of the sympathetic public. The formality of a trial, of course, had to be gone through, but she had already been acquitted by a jury of her peers—twelve of Broadway's most radiant ladies of the stage.

The New York *World* reported it thus:

JURY OF STAGE WOMEN DECLARES NAN PATTERSON INNOCENT. MANY OF THEM KNOW HER PERSONALLY, CALL HER A GENTLE GIRL AND SEE NO REASON WHY SHE SHOULD HAVE KILLED YOUNG

HERE'S THE JURY THAT VOTES NAN PATTERSON "NOT GUILTY"

Emma Carus	*Indianola Arnold*
Cherida Simpson	*Vaughan Sargeant*
Ida Brooks Hunt	*Mal Leslie*
Lillian Coleman	*Ida Mantell*
Edna Goodrich	*May McKenzie*
Vivian Blackburn	*Bonnie Maginn*

These glamorous ladies were interviewed at length by the *World*. They displayed a remarkable familiarity with the evidence, which established conclusively to their minds that Young must have shot himself. They were all convinced that Nan was a gentle girl who would not harm a fly. What her attitude was toward bookmakers they did not say.

It is too much to hope that the jurors who were subsequently to determine Nan's fate did not read this, for everybody was reading everything about the case. Today a journalistic stunt such as this would bring down a storm of censure. Standards, happily, have improved. In England an offending editor would be sentenced to a heavy fine and a long term in prison.

But this was fifty-four years ago and the Hearst-Pulitzer conflict was raging at its yellowest. District Attorney Jerome and his cohorts were busily preparing their case—interviewing witnesses, studying anatomy, examining pistol experts and hunting for the Smiths. His opponents were equally active in getting ready for the defense, particularly in the field where it counted most—in the newspapers.

In August Nan was still sighing for green fields and the bright sunlight, so her lawyers again sued out a writ of habeas corpus which came on for hearing before Supreme Court Justice Amend. After a mild opposition by the district attorney, Justice Amend fixed $20,000 bail and it seemed for a while to the jubilant press that Nan would be promptly released. But the bail could not be raised and her lawyers decided that no further efforts would be made to free her before the trial. The district attorney agreed to bring on the case in the fall and at length the date of November fifteenth was agreed upon.

This was the lull before the battle, but the public still was not deprived of its daily quota of news. Interspersed among items about Nan's ailing mother, her offers of marriage, and stories that prominent theatrical producers were bidding for her services as soon as she was released—it was reported that a play called "The Mystery of the Hansom Cab" was being written for her—a new topic of momentous importance was introduced: What would Nan wear in court?

There were repeated reports that a fashionable dressmaker was visiting the Tombs to create a suitable wardrobe for the ordeal that lay ahead. These reports Mr. Levy indignantly denied. "There will be no theatrical display of any kind," he said. "Miss Patterson will wear a simple, black silk gown. She hasn't the means to do anything else. If she had I wouldn't allow it."

The reporters seem to have been able to wander in and out of the Tombs with a freedom that no longer exists in these more restrained times. One of them visited Nan and interviewed her on November fourteenth, the day before the trial.

> "Just see how stout I have grown in prison," she said to an *Evening World* reporter today. "Why, my friends who haven't seen me and think I have been wasting away will be amazed when they see how rotund I have become. I looked over my dresses to see what I would wear for the trial, and I finally picked one, but would you believe it, I couldn't get it on, I've got so fat. So I had to have a new one, and my dressmaker was here this morning and will be here this afternoon to fit it. It's just a plain black gown with a white front to the waist. I don't want to wear anything flashy, but I am anxious to make a good appearance."

So that there may be no doubt about this important matter let it be recorded that when Nan entered court the following morning she wore "a new gown of black voile cut with a full skirt, and wore a black picture hat adorned with a large black ostrich plume and a heavy veil." The newspaper pictures show that she also wore black gloves. Just what the well-dressed homicide defendant should wear!

CHAPTER TWELVE

The Trial Begins

On the morning of November 15, 1904, the case of the People versus Nan Patterson for murder in the first degree was called for trial in the Criminal Term of the Supreme Court. For hours before the opening of court a vast crowd had gathered in the corridors of the old Criminal Courts Building, clamoring for admission. Shortly before the doors of the courtroom opened, additional police reserves had to be summoned to keep the unruly crowd under control.

A few minutes before ten o'clock Nan walked across the Bridge of Sighs that joined the courthouse and the Tombs, the Via Dolorosa over which so many unfortunates had passed during the sordid history of the old building. She was pale but self-possessed, and she wore the black voile dress and the picture hat that have been described above. Her old father, he of the drooping whiskers, arose from the counsel table where he was seated, and they embraced affectionately, a ritual that was to be repeated each day until the end. It is certain that the effect of this filial scene was not lost upon the newspaper people, the spectators and the talesmen who jammed the courtroom.

At ten-thirty, to the accompaniment of the traditional "Oyez! Oyez!" Mr. Justice Vernon M. Davis, who was to preside at the trial, black-robed and dignified, entered and took his seat beneath the mural paintings of Justice, the Fates, and Liberty, Fraternity and Equality that adorned the wall behind the bench.

Judge Davis was a tall, handsome man who was later to become a respected member of the Appellate Division of the Supreme Court. He had formerly been an assistant district attorney, and he was highly regarded in the legal profession for his fairness and his knowledge of criminal law. He was an excellent choice to preside over an important case.

At the defense table sat Nan with her father and her counsel, Mr. Levy, Mr. Unger, and Daniel O'Reilly, a young former assistant district attorney who had been engaged to assist in the preparation of the defense.

At the prosecutor's table sat District Attorney Jerome and his two star assistants, William Rand and Francis Garvan. William Travers Jerome was a vigorous, energetic man who had been a judge, and who had vaulted into fame as a crusading reformer by personally leading raids upon brothels and gambling houses. It was said that he had Presidential ambitions.

Jerome had a young English cousin who also had political aspirations—a young fellow named Winston Churchill who was beginning to come up in public life. If the subject had ever arisen at the time, prophets would have bet that William

Travers had a better chance of reaching the White House than young cousin Winston had of ever living at 10 Downing Street. But one of the obstacles in Jerome's path to glory was the plump, comely figure of Nan Patterson, and it was important that her case should be prosecuted to a successful conclusion.

Jerome did not participate in the trial of Nan Patterson, although he was in court nearly every day. He had entrusted the task of prosecuting the case to his ace assistant, William Rand, who at the age of thirty-eight was then at the top of his splendid form as an advocate.

Rand had been born in Chicago of wealthy parents. After the Chicago fire his father had taken the family to Europe, where they remained for five years, and where the boy had attended school at Vevey and Dresden. Upon his return to America he studied with a private tutor and then entered Phillips Exeter Academy. Then followed Harvard College, *cum laude,* and three years at Harvard Law School, from which he was graduated *summa cum laude.* In 1895 he was appointed an assistant corporation counsel of New York City, where he quickly became one of the leading trial assistants. In 1902 Jerome appointed him to his staff.

Rand was a formidable opponent. His principal weakness as an advocate—as the present writer, who once tried a case against him, can testify—was a supercilious, condescending manner that did not ingratiate him with New York juries. Alexander Woollcott said of him, "He was a brilliant advocate, although in talking to a jury . . . he did rather suggest an English squire addressing the tenantry."

A stranger contrast, in both appearance and manner, can

hardly be imagined than that which existed between the two adversaries. Rand was tall and athletic. He wore his hair parted in the middle in the Richard Harding Davis style that was fashionable in those days, and, with his jutting jaw, he was the prototype of that long procession of relentless prosecutors whom the motion pictures have made part of American mythology.

Levy, short, stout and bald, had a benign suavity that made him resemble, to quote Woollcott, a cherub. "Mr. Levy," Woollcott continues, "managed to suggest that he was just a shabby neighbor of the jurors, trying to rescue a fluttering butterfly from the juggernaut of the State."

A jury was impaneled with difficulty, but at length twelve good men and true were found who swore that they would have no scruples about sending Nan to the electric chair if the evidence warranted it. Mr. Rand opened his case to the jury and then proceeded to present his evidence.

Thanksgiving fell on November twenty-fourth, but the holiday did not interrupt the torrent of news about Nan that continued to flood the compassionate pages of the newspapers, all of which, we can be sure, was read by the jurors.

Thus we read that Nan declined the elaborate Thanksgiving dinner her friends wanted to send her and elected unselfishly to dine with the other women prisoners—a frugal repast (the menu was printed in a box on the first page of the *World*) consisting of oxtail soup, turkey stuffed with chestnuts, cranberry sauce, stewed tomatoes, mince pie, ice cream and coffee.

The hearts of the jurors must have bled as they read that evening the pathetic note Nan had received in the morning from her ailing mother. "We expected you to be home for Thanksgiving," she wrote, "but there can be no thanks giving for us until you are free."

A little six-year-old girl in Washington wrote, "Try to keep up your spirits and keep well." Another letter came from San Francisco, and a telegram arrived from a wealthy woman (name undisclosed) reading: "Don't lose courage. God is with you."

Nan was showered with gifts on Thanksgiving Day, including three four-leaf clovers, one in a beautiful glass case framed in gold. "Here is good luck," she exclaimed as she showed it to the reporters who accidentally happened to be standing in the vicinity. "How good it makes me feel to think that so many persons still love and trust me." She also received a big basket of fruit and a five-pound box of candy from someone who signed himself "A Sympathizer." These gifts she generously shared with her companions who were being detained in the Tombs on less romantic charges.

Several baskets and bouquets of flowers arrived at the Tombs but were refused by the authorities in compliance with a rule banning flowers to persons charged with a capital crime because it tended to make heroes of them. Apparently the rule did not apply to candy and fruit.

The jurors who read about Nan's sad holiday were undoubtedly moved most of all by the stories of Nan's devotion to the little eleven-month-old De Pietro baby. Mrs. De Pietro was also being held on a murder charge, and the child was living in the Tombs with her. Mrs. De Pietro had shot and killed a scoundrel who had tried to seduce her away from her husband. But poor Mrs. De Pietro had never been in Rector's, had never been on the stage, and had probably never been in a hansom cab. As the mother gratefully partook of Nan's munificence, Nan fondled and petted the baby to the great delight of the visiting press. It was a touching manifestation of the maternal instinct.

"Yes," said Nan's father to the reporters, "Nan and the baby are great friends. She has taught it to call me 'Papa' and Nan usually brings the baby down with her to the matron's room every morning when she comes to see me."

On the morning of November twenty-sixth (Judge Davis was holding Saturday sessions to expedite the trial), the court was informed that Juror Number Nine, Edward J. Dressler, had had a cerebral hemorrhage and was paralyzed. The following Monday Judge Davis declared a mistrial and dismissed the jury. He announced that the new trial would commence the following Monday.

Nan was disconsolate at the prospect of going through the ordeal a second time, but, except for a mild attack of tonsillitis, she managed to bear up and devote herself to her literary endeavors, all of which was duly reported. Nan, during her confinement, had taken to breaking into poetry, and one of the gems was preserved for posterity by the press:

> Life's highest hope, its sweetest peace,
> Is ours, can we forget,
> And mend the broken, sorrowed past
> Whose memoirs spell regret.
>
> The fairest rose conceals a thorn,
> And after pleasure, pain;
> And happy some, and some forlorn,
> Yet life is not in vain.

> The cross is heavy and hard to bear
> And narrow the way and straight,
> Your life is e'er self-sacrifice,
> Don't learn the lesson late.

There was widespread compassion for the fragile chorus girl who was about to be subjected to the agony of a second trial, and there was speculation among her sporting friends who nightly gathered at the Metropole bar as to whether or not there was some sort of jinx on the case. Gamblers are notoriously superstitious, as the New York *American,* in its zeal for accuracy, pointed out, and there had been an uncanny succession of calamities. Nan's mother had been stricken by a heart attack; Hyman Stern, the pawnbroker, had been operated on for appendicitis; during the first trial the mother-in-law of Edward Hendricks, the foreman of the jury, had died; and now the unfortunate Juror Dressler was paralyzed. (The *American* neglected to mention that Nan had had tonsillitis and, for that matter, Caesar Young had had a bullet shot into his chest.) The coincidences were too striking to be passed over as accidental.

At the Metropole bar they pondered over the possible cause of these catastrophes. One bookmaker ascribed it to the skeleton that was used at the trial. He told tales of what ills had befallen those who had desecrated the bones of the dead. . . . Another ascribed the seeming ill luck to the rabbit's foot that rumor declared Roland B. Molineux had carried during his trial and had lately given to the accused actress, those wise in tokens and charms declaring that where the rabbit's foot might have boded good luck for Molineux it would, in the next case, mean bad luck. . . .

CHAPTER THIRTEEN

Nan Takes the Stand

On DECEMBER 5, 1904, Nan Patterson again went on trial. The public had been whipped into a frenzy and the police had difficulty preventing the crowds that thronged the corridors from crashing into the courtroom.

Once again Nan, still dressed in somber black, went through the daily ritual of kissing her old father upon her arrival in court in the morning and her departure in the afternoon. The Russo-Japanese War was raging and Port Arthur was in imminent danger of falling, but to the metropolitan press Nan Patterson was the paramount news of the day.

With painstaking thoroughness Rand built up a powerful case of circumstantial evidence against the defendant. As the procession of witnesses, police officers, doctors and pistol experts passed before the jury, Levy, with all the skill at his command, tried to break down the impact of their testimony by cross-examination.

The Smiths were still missing. Pawnbroker Stern was unable to identify Nan as the woman who had accompanied the purchaser of the gun. But Rand had saved his strongest evidence—the letter that Julia Smith had written to Young—until the end of the prosecution's case.

Levy, backed up by the legal erudition of his partner, Henry Unger, fought valorously to keep the letter out. It was a close question and it was not until Judge Davis conferred with some of his colleagues on the Supreme Court that he decided to admit it in evidence. Its admission was generally regarded as a severe defeat for the defense, and many of Nan's most optimistic supporters began to have misgivings as to her fate.

With the reading to the jury of the letter in which Julia had written that Nan "might do something either serious to you or herself," Rand rested his case. The customary motions to dismiss were made and denied and the court took a recess until the afternoon.

For weeks there had been speculation in the newspapers and around the courthouse whether Nan would dare become a witness in her own behalf. Rand's reputation as a cross-examiner was well known and few believed that the defendant would have the courage to face him or the skill to cope with him. If there was uncertainty in the defense camp it is my guess that the decision to call Nan was forced by the devastating effect of the Julia Smith letter.

At 2:30 in the afternoon Levy rose and said, "Miss Patterson, will you please take the stand."

There was a tense stillness in the crowded courtroom as Nan rose from the counsel table where she was seated, kissed her father and walked slowly to the witness stand. She was pale, and it was evident that she was under a great strain. She placed her hand upon the Bible that the clerk held out to her and swore to tell the truth, the whole truth, and nothing but the truth, so help her God.

"Miss Patterson," her lawyer said when she was seated in the witness chair, "will you please remove your hat." She removed her large picture hat with the ostrich plume and looked out at the audience that faced her. On the bench, beside Judge Davis, sat the Earl of Suffolk, who was in America to be married to an heiress and who was determined not to miss the most gripping show of the generation.

As her counsel began his direct examination the defendant answered in a low, well-modulated voice that was clearly audible to the jurors and the reporters.

Q. What is your full name?
A. Nan Randolph Patterson.
Q. You have been married?
A. Yes, to Leon Gaines Martin.
Q. How old are you?
A. Twenty-three.
Q. Your next birthday will be when?
A. On September twenty-third next.
Q. When was it that you were married, Nan?
A. In 1898.
Q. You have been divorced?
A. Yes.
Q. Now I wish you to try and not be nervous. When did you go to California?
A. In the summer of 1903.
Q. Was it there that you met Caesar Young?
A. On the way to California.
Q. What business were you in?

A. In the theatrical business.

Q. Your relations with Caesar Young continued after you met him?

A. Yes.

Q. How long after you met him was your divorce procured?

A. About a year.

Q. Did Young secure the divorce for you?

Mr. Rand was on his feet. "I object," he shouted.

Q. At whose suggestion was the divorce secured?

A. Mr. Young's.

Q. When did you leave the Coast to come East the last time?

A. I came in March for the last time.

The direct examination took Nan through the occurrences after her arrival in New York, all of which have been recounted—the visit to the races on June third, her meeting with Young that night, and the fatal ride downtown the following morning in the hansom cab.

It was after five o'clock, more than three hours later, when Mr. Levy, with his flair for the dramatic, said, "Nan, look at me. Did you shoot Caesar Young?"

"I did not," she replied, returning his gaze steadily. "I swear I did not. God knows if I could bring him back to life I would!"

"That is all," said Mr. Levy. It was a perfect curtain line and the court adjourned until the following morning. Everyone agreed that she had been a good witness, but this was just the prelude as she was led through the gentle paths of direct examination by the sympathetic questioning of her own lawyer. Her great ordeal lay ahead. Tomorrow would be Rand's day.

We can be sure that the prosecutor's staff was busy that night studying the stenographic minutes of Nan's testimony to find ammunition for Rand's cross-examination. It should be said that, in spite of stories to the contrary, the defense throughout the trial was handicapped by lack of funds. Each night the district attorney received a stenographic transcript of the day's testimony, an invaluable aid in the preparation of a case. But the defense did not have the money to pay for the minutes and was obliged to rely upon the notes taken by counsel.

The following day the biggest crowd to date clamored to get into the court. "In its closing hours," said the *Times,* "the trial is attracting an attention which has tested the recollection of court regulars for a precedent. The police in the corridor were busy an hour before court opened in fighting back would-be spectators. Among the curious who sought admission were many women. They were all told that they would not be allowed entrance but refused to accept the ruling, and it was noticeable when Justice Davis ascended the bench that they had carried their point, for several women had seats at both the morning and afternoon session.

"The cross-examination of the defendant was begun immediately upon the opening of court," the *Times* continued. "When she took the stand, after a moment spent in the chair beside her father, she kissed him as if she were bidding him goodbye. She did not remove her hat, as on her direct examination, but her veil was thrown back and her face was in the plain view of the jury."

Rand launched into his cross-examination at once. "When

you left Los Angeles for the East, did Young give you any money?" he asked.

A. He gave me $2,800.

Q. Was that for a two weeks' trip?

A. I was only away from him for two weeks.

Q. How much money did Young give you altogether?

A. I don't know.

Q. Was it as much as $15,000?

A. I do not remember.

Q. Was it as much as $40,000 or $50,000?

A. I don't know.

Young, the witness said, had been very generous toward her. She had not worked since she met Young early in 1903. Her father was not wealthy and did not provide for her, but Young had been liberal. Twenty-eight hundred dollars, she thought, was the largest amount he had ever given her, but on one occasion he gave her $2,500 and at other times he had given her sums from $1,000 to $1,500. Young, she said, was extremely lavish and spent as much money on his friends as he did on himself.

Q. He gave you money whenever you wanted it?

A. Yes.

Q. At the race track on the afternoon of June third, Young told you they had trapped him?

A. Yes.

Q. What did he mean by trapped?

A. That his folks had bought tickets for him and that he had to go. He couldn't get out of it.

Q. Did he speak of his wife's happiness as a reason why he should go abroad?

A. He said his wife was happy to go.

Then Rand opened up a new line of testimony.

Q. Did Young ever say to you that his wife might become a murderess if he did not sever his relations with you?

A. He said he was afraid that his wife would kill me or kill him. He said she was armed. That was on the day I met him at the races. He recalled something that had happened in San Francisco.

Q. As a matter of fact did Young ever tell you that he feared his wife might kill him?

A. He never did.

Q. Was he afraid that while his wife was in Europe she might kill you in America?

A. No.

Q. Were you feeling in good spirits on the night of June third?

A. Yes.

Q. You loved him passionately, devoutly; he was the one man in the world for you?

A. Yes.

Q. And he was going away on the morrow with his wife?

A. Yes.

Q. And still you were happy, knowing that he was going away?

A. I knew that he was going away, but I did not think he would be away long.

Q. You had no idea of going after him?

A. No.

Q. Were you ever in Europe?

A. No.

Q. Why did you not wish to go abroad?

A. I was afraid of the trip.

Q. You had crossed the continent by yourself and had been at hotels alone.

A. Yes.

Q. Did you want a chaperone?

A. No.

I have already quoted Nan's testimony relating to the events on the fatal June fourth. When Rand came to the point where she said that Young had seized her hand, he re-enacted the scene, assisted by Mr. Garvan, with Nan directing it from the witness chair.

"Did you ever give your lawyers any of the letters that Young wrote to you?" Rand then asked. The witness said that she had not.

"Mr. Levy," said Rand, "I now request you to keep your promise and produce the letters which passed between Young and the defendant last winter in California."

"You must be in terrible straits," Levy replied blandly.

"Miss Patterson," said Rand, turning to the witness, "are you willing that I should put Mr. Levy on the stand and question him as to Young's letters to you?"

"I am."

"And to waive your rights and privileges in this regard?"

Mr. Levy rose to object to this and sternly advised his client that she was to waive none of her rights and privileges. He was running this case, he said, and would conduct it according to his own judgment.

Rand was stymied. He asked Nan a few questions about the

letter Julia Smith had written to Young, and she disclaimed any knowledge of it. That ended the cross-examination.

When Nan returned to her seat she was deathly pale and she whispered to her lawyer that she wished to leave the courtroom for a moment. Mr. Levy urged her to control herself, and shortly after that the court took a recess.

The afternoon session was brief. Mr. Levy called a clerk from Bellevue Hospital to testify that there had been an accident at the 34th Street ferry house on the afternoon of June third and that the street had been blocked. Rand recalled Mrs. Young, who had previously been a witness, and asked her a few unimportant questions. The State then rested its case.

It was a shrewd move to call Young's widow as the last witness. Rand undoubtedly did it so that the final picture left in the minds of the jurors would be that of the wronged, bereaved wife and not that of her young, attractive rival who had just left the stand.

The newspapers and spectators were in unanimous agreement that Nan had withstood her cross-examination well. She had been under a frightening strain but at all times had kept herself under perfect control. To one reading her testimony it seems that she was an ideal witness, never evasive, answering the questions briefly and to the point. The following morning the *Times* said:

> Nan Patterson, the chorus girl accused of the murder of Caesar Young, bore herself bravely on cross-examination yesterday, and did not falter a single time under the fire of Assistant District Attorney Rand's pitiless questioning. She was on the stand for two hours and a quarter.

CHAPTER FOURTEEN

"He That Is Without Sin . . ."

ON THE FOLLOWING DAY the lawyers summed up to the jury, and the crowd that tried to storm its way into the court to hear the final scene of the drama was the largest yet. The *Times* said:

> There was an unusually large crowd about the doors of the courtroom when they swung open for the morning session and no little confusion resulted. It was during the recess hour, however, that the real rush occurred. Men and women fought for admission as if their lives depended upon gaining entrance. The police were almost swept from their feet. Any and every excuse was urged to get inside. When all failed, offers of money were freely made. Not once but a dozen times did women try to buy their way in, offering sums from $1 to $10. Extra chairs were brought from all parts of the building, and before Justice Davis ascended the bench the aisles were almost blocked. Before two o'clock, the hour fixed for reconvening the court, it was necessary to clear the cor-

ridors on the first floor. Until adjournment was taken the police were beleaguered and compelled to resort to force to keep the crowd back.

Mr. Levy's speech was a skillful blend of logic and emotional appeal and for three hours he held the jurors spellbound. The climax was reached when he picked up a New Testament from the table before him and in his rich, beautifully cadenced voice read the story of the woman taken in adultery. "He that is without sin among you, let him cast a stone at her . . . When Jesus had lifted up himself and saw none but the woman he said unto her, 'Woman, where are thine accusers? Hath no man condemned thee?' She said, 'No man, Lord.' And Jesus said unto her, 'Neither do I condemn thee. Go and sin no more.' "

Mr. Levy stood in silence for a moment and then walked slowly to his seat. From the rear of the courtroom sobs could be heard from the audience. I know, for I had cut school that day and I was there.

It was a grand, dramatic finish. Corny? Perhaps, according to present-day standards, but this was 1904 and the vogue of tear-jerking oratory had not yet become outmoded in the courts. Mr. Rand's speech that followed was a masterpiece of logic and forceful presentation. I was, of course, rooting ardently for an acquittal, but as I sat there enthralled by that superb oration, I found myself being persuaded of Nan's guilt in spite of myself.

To Rand a jury was a collective intellect to be reasoned with and convinced. To Levy it was something beyond that: it was a musical instrument to be played upon with virtuoso skill. I have often wondered whether Rand's brilliant marshaling of the evidence had as much impact upon the twelve men in the jury box as that moving reading from the Gospel, the fact that Christmas was just a few days off—a circumstance that Levy did not neglect to mention—and the sight of the frail magdalen, sitting pale-faced beside her aged father.

The newspaper men, more hard-boiled than the jurors, were more profoundly impressed, as indeed I was, by Mr. Rand's speech than by Mr. Levy's. The *Times* said the following day:

> The distinct feature of yesterday's proceeding was the address of Assistant District Attorney Rand. For more than three hours and a half he held the breathless attention of the jury, invoking satire, epigram, and logic in hammering at the case of the defense. As he put forth point after point the entire audience—and the courtroom was packed as it had seldom been before—fairly hung upon his words.

The greatest compliment that Rand received was paid to him by his adversary. "In all my twenty-four years' experience at the New York bar," Levy said, "I have never heard such a speech. It was a marvel of advocacy. Despite its effect, however, I expect an acquittal in all confidence." Mr. Levy knew a good speech when he heard one; but he also knew juries.

The next morning Justice Davis delivered his charge—it was generally agreed that it was "a model of fairness"—and at about noon the jurors retired to deliberate on Nan's fate. By now popular excitement had reached a pitch bordering upon hysteria. The *Times* said:

> Not in years have such crowds awaited a verdict in any case. When court was opened yesterday morning the rush for admission was so great that in less than five minutes it was necessary to close the doors, and until midnight last night the Criminal Courts Building was invested with great throngs of the curious who blocked the streets and refused to move

> although the police, under the command of Inspector Titus, made every effort to keep the thoroughfares open. . . .
>
> The noon recess brought no decrease in the crowds about the courtroom. The public was excluded, the police denying access even to the building unless those who sought entrance had business within. At three o'clock the street in front of the building was packed from curb to curb. There were many women in the throng. Franklin Street, beneath the Bridge of Sighs, was impassable.

The newspapers reported that Sir Charles Wyndham, the noted English actor, lost his pocketbook in the crush.

At 11:25 that night, after deliberating eleven hours, the jury reported that they had not agreed and Justice Davis ordered them locked up for the night. Today it is customary to provide comfortable hotel accommodations for a jury that has to be locked up, but in 1904 that humane provision did not exist. The jurors had to spend the night in the jury room, sleeping as best they could on the uncomfortable cane chairs. There were no cots provided, and the next day the solicitous newspapers expressed great concern for the health of some of the elderly jurors.

The following morning the jury resumed its deliberations and about noon the foreman sent word they were hopelessly deadlocked. Justice Davis sent for them and discharged them.

The first major battle was over. The popular feeling was that Nan had scored a victory, and that she would never be convicted. The jury had stood six for conviction and six for acquittal.

CHAPTER FIFTEEN

Enter the Smiths and Recorder Goff

THERE HAD BEEN weaknesses in Rand's case, one of the greatest being his inability to prove the identity of the man and the woman who had bought the revolver in Hyman Stern's pawnshop on June third. Stern had sworn that Nan, to the best of his recollection, was not the woman, but the couple might have been Julia and Morgan Smith. Stern's clerk had testified that he believed the pistol had been sold about six o'clock in the evening, and the keystone of Rand's theory was that Morgan Smith was the man who had bought it.

Early in March 1905 the prosecutor got the break he had long waited for: the elusive Smiths were discovered in Toronto. Hyman Stern, accompanied by a detective, was at once rushed up to Canada, but when he arrived there the birds had flown.

Stern, however, had just barely missed seeing Morgan Smith, who was enjoying the luxury of a morning shave when the door of the barbershop opened and Stern and the detective entered. Smith may have seen and recognized Stern in the mirror, for, as it will later appear, he had on several occasions patronized Stern's pawnshop. To the astonishment of the startled barber he jumped from the chair and dashed out of the shop through a side door, the lather still on his face.

Smith had become friendly in Toronto with a young Canadian detective named T. H. Aiken, who had tipped off the New York authorities as to the Smiths' whereabouts. Smith knew he was a detective but was naïvely under the impression that he was working on some other case. The two men had become extremely intimate, so when Smith decided abruptly to move on his new friend suggested that he accompany him.

Smith and his wife and the detective, after their hurried departure from Toronto, visited several Canadian cities and then returned to the United States. After a brief stay in Detroit they went to Cleveland, where Smith left his wife at a hotel and then, together with the detective, journeyed south.

By this time he was running short of funds and he concluded that he had better look for work, so he visited Louisville and then Nashville in the hope of getting a job with some of the bookmakers there. But no job was to be found, so he wired his wife to meet him in Cincinnati. They registered at the Grand Hotel as "H. H. Banning and Wife," and their faithful friend, the detective, who had taken a room at the same hotel, went out and sent a telegram to District Attorney Jerome:

> SMITH AND JULIA ARE AT THE GRAND HOTEL. WIRE INSTRUCTIONS.

The district attorney immediately replied:

> ARREST SMITH AND WIFE AS FUGITIVES FROM JUSTICE. THE GOVERNOR'S WARRANT WILL FOLLOW AS SOON AS IT IS POSSIBLE TO PROCURE IT.

The district attorney, as soon as he heard that the Smiths had been discovered, went before the Grand Jury and obtained an indictment against them for conspiracy to extort money from Young. Just what was the nature of the conspiracy is not quite clear, and it is apparent that the indictment was intended principally as a device to enable the prosecutor to bring them back to New York and keep them locked up during the trial. Smith, of course, was guilty of contempt of court in disobeying a Grand Jury subpoena, but contempt is not an extraditable offense. Conspiracy is. Besides, Rand wanted Julia as well as Morgan.

The Smiths were promptly arrested in Cincinnati; they waived extradition and were hustled back to New York and lodged in the Tombs. Through the kindness of the warden Julia was placed in a cell near Nan's and for the first time since the day of the shooting the two sisters met. "How much older you look!" Nan exclaimed. "You do too," Julia replied. There is little wonder. Nearly a year had passed and both girls had been through a lot.

The prosecution was, of course, elated at the arrest. One might have expected that there would have been consternation in the camp of the defense, but astonishingly their gratification equaled that of the prosecution. The exuberant Mr. Levy was, according to the newspapers, as happy about the return of the Smiths as Mr. Rand was. "This was the only thing we still needed," he said to the reporters. "Now the mystery will surely be cleared up. This arrest makes it more certain that before that we shall secure a verdict of not guilty for our client." Since the return of Morgan and Julia caused so much rejoicing all around, one is surprised at their lack of consideration in staying away so long.

But in spite of Levy's brave words, the capture of the Smiths was—or might be—a severe blow to the defense. If Hyman Stern should identify Morgan Smith as the purchaser of the revolver, Nan's chances would be very poor. When the news of the arrest of the Smiths reached the lobby of the Hotel Metropole, the betting odds on Nan's ultimate liberation dropped sharply. Caesar Young's former cronies, as an appropriate tribute to his memory, were making book on the outcome of the case.

Rand was now almost ready to try his case—but not quite. At last Pawnbroker Stern would be brought face to face with Morgan Smith. But a judge still had to be found who could be counted upon to see that Nan did not have the slightest chance of slipping through the meshes of the law. This was a vital part of the prosecution's preparation for trial. The judge in a criminal case is the most important actor in the entire performance. He controls the admission and exclusion of evidence; he can shut counsel off peremptorily; and, most important of all, his words and behavior have a powerful influence upon a jury of laymen. The lawyers, jurors say, are partisan, but the learned jurist in the silk robe on the bench is fair and impartial. This, regrettably, is not always true.

The judge whom the district attorney chose to assist Nan on her journey to the electric chair was Recorder John W. Goff of the Court of General Sessions,* the cruelest, most sadistic judge we have had in New York in this century. Rand was taking no chances this time. The case had been pending in the Criminal Term of Supreme Court, but the transfer to Goff's court was a simple matter. The district attorney had the power then, and still has, to juggle cases about to suit his purpose.

Goff had become celebrated as counsel to the famous Lexow Committee that in the nineties had exposed the sinister tie-up between Tammany and vice and corruption. On the strength of the reputation he had won as an enemy of sin he had been elected in 1895 a judge of the Court of General Sessions, the oldest court in the country. Here he quickly became a terror, not only to the unfortunate criminals who were tried before him, but to any defendant or lawyer who had the misfortune to appear in his court.

Goff's age was problematical. He had been born in Ireland and had come to this country in his youth. After he had served for many years in General Sessions he was promoted (some time after the Nan Patterson trial) to the Supreme Court, and when he seemed to be approaching the constitutional retirement age of seventy years he gave no indication of any intention to relinquish his judicial office. This was a matter of concern for the New York bar, who wanted to get rid of him, so a committee of lawyers was sent to Ireland to find out how old he was. There they learned that the parish church in which he had been baptized had burned down and all the records

* Recorder was the title bestowed upon the senior judge of the Court of General Sessions, an ancient court whose history goes back to the Dutch days of New York City. The title was abolished some years ago and Goff was the last Recorder.

had been destroyed, so Goff stayed on until it suited him to retire.

Recorder Goff was a handsome and imposing figure on the bench. His head was framed in an aureole of silver hair, and his silken beard with a sheen of spun silver, his ruddy cheeks, and his piercing blue eyes made him resemble a medieval portrait of a saint. Mr. Levy always referred to him privately as "that saintlike s.o.b."

I heard Goff in court many times, and in my younger days I appeared before him on several occasions. He used to speak in a low voice, almost a whisper, but he could make himself heard when he wanted to. When he charged a jury in a criminal case, it sounded something like this: "Whst, whst, whst, GUILTY! . . . Whst, whst, whst, GUILTY! . . . Whst, whst, whst, GUILTY!" It did not matter if the jurors understood anything else he said; that one word uttered with the explosive force of a rifle shot was burned indelibly in their minds.

Lest it may seem that my description of Goff is unfair, let me quote a great lawyer who often appeared before him. The late Lloyd Paul Stryker in his book *The Art of Advocacy* says of Goff:

> He had a cold heart and a sadistic joy in suffering. . . . The judge who had seemed a saint was now revealed as one intent on striking down a fellow citizen no matter how. From his face the mask of benignity was soon laid aside, and as I gazed up at the bench I felt like some four-footed denizen of the jungle that suddenly stares into the cold visage of a python. . . .
>
> He shared with Jeffreys what Macaulay called "the most

> odious vice which is incident to human nature, a delight in misery as mere misery."

Stryker was writing this about the celebrated trial of Lieutenant Charles Becker in which he had participated as associate counsel for the defense and over which Goff had presided. In that case the Court of Appeals, New York's highest court, said: ". . . the defendant certainly was entitled to a scrupulously fair trial where nothing should be done to prejudice his case. . . . We do not think that the defendant had such a trial." And Judge Miller, in a concurring opinion, said the verdict was "shockingly against the weight of evidence . . . because the trial was so conducted as to insure a verdict of guilty regardless of the evidence."

One factor that contributed to Goff's irascibility was a stomach ailment. His daily lunch consisted of a bowl of crackers and milk, but this frugal repast was supplemented, so Mr. Levy told me, by a bottle of Irish whisky that he used to keep beneath the bench in court and from which, at intervals, he would take a generous swig. This undoubtedly accounted for the cherubic pink complexion that added so much to his benign appearance.

His inability to eat a substantial meal, and his yogilike endurance, fortified with Irish whisky, made him utterly inconsiderate of the physical needs of the others in his court. During the Becker case he compelled John F. McIntyre, Becker's chief counsel, to conduct an important examination, with only a half-hour recess at noon, until eight-thirty at night, allowing no time out for food or even the calls of nature. McIntyre, who was on the verge of collapse, had to terminate his cross-examination unfinished, and this was one of the grounds upon which the Court of Appeals reversed

Becker's conviction. Goff had done the same thing ten years earlier in the Nan Patterson case.

This was the judge chosen by the prosecutor to help him convict Nan Patterson. As we shall presently see, there were occasions during the trial when he did not quite live up to the prosecutor's expectations. Not that Goff was fair; he was temperamentally incapable of that. But many of his rulings, particularly on certain critical questions of evidence, were definitely favorable to the defense.

Why any judge behaves the way he does is one of those mysteries that lawyers spend a lifetime trying to understand. Why Goff, in the Nan Patterson case, acted with even a semblance of judicial fairness toward the defendant is a matter of speculation. I have two explanations. One is that there was, as I faintly recall, a bitter feud between Goff and Jerome, and I remember hearing that on one occasion Goff had fined Jerome for contempt of court.

Another reason that seems plausible to me is that Goff, who had come from humble Irish stock, was not sympathetic with the haughty, Ivy League manner of Mr. Rand. Whatever the reason, Nan might have fared much worse as she entered court to undergo for the third time the ordeal of trial by jury.

CHAPTER SIXTEEN

The Last Round Begins

THE THIRD TRIAL of Nan Patterson began on April 18, 1905, in Part Two of the Court of General Sessions. The same crowds that had attended the first two trials were there again, clamoring for admission, and again police reserves had to be hurried to the courthouse to maintain order.

As Judge Goff took his seat on the bench and Rand arose to move, for the third time, the case of the People of the State of New York versus Nan Patterson a noticeable change was observed at the counsel table. Nan's ancient father was no longer seated there beside his daughter. Recorder Goff, with a regrettable disregard for paternal affection and the artistic requirements of stagecraft, had directed that the old gentleman must henceforth sit outside the railing among the spectators. This time Nan was not dressed in black as she had been at the first two trials. She wore a becoming steel-gray dress that had been specially made for this trial. Second mourning, I suppose.

A large panel of talesmen had been summoned, and at the end of the first day three jurors had been accepted. This was remarkably fast work, considering that there was probably not a man or woman in the country who had not read about the case and had not formed an opinion about it.

However, Goff was not satisfied. The following morning he announced that the jury had to be impaneled that day and that he would sit until the job was completed. The lawyers on both sides, faced with the grim prospect of working continuously around the clock, apparently curtailed their accustomed verbosity, and at 7:45 that night the twelfth juror was sworn in and took his seat in the box. It just shows that it can be done.

The testimony started with the customary dull preliminaries, the introduction in evidence of photographs, diagrams, maps and the like, but the testimony of Joseph Ireland, architect and surveyor, is worth pausing over. For Ireland had made detailed scale drawings of the hansom cab in which Caesar Young had been shot.

For the benefit of those readers who are too young to remember that picturesque vehicle of a bygone day, the description and statistics as given by Ireland are necessary to an understanding of this case.

The hansom cab was a two-wheeled conveyance that somewhat resembled a coffin standing on end. Perched up on top, in the rear, was the driver in a sort of crow's nest. The reins extended over the top of the cab to the horse out in front. In the roof of the cab was a small trap door which was kept closed unless the driver and the passenger wanted to communicate with each other.

The passengers sat facing the horse, and the front side of the cab was open. There were, however, two folding doors which could be opened and closed by the driver. When they were closed they reached about to the chest of the passenger. On each side of the cab in the back were small glass windows.

To be specific, here are the figures given by Mr. Ireland: The distance from the seat to the top of the cab was three feet eight inches; the distance from the seat to the floor was seventeen inches; and the seat was three feet wide and sixteen inches deep. The doors were two feet ten inches from the floor, and when they were closed there was about eleven inches of space between them and the occupants.

It will be seen, therefore, that however Caesar Young died, whether by murder or suicide, the tragedy was enacted in a space not much larger than a telephone booth.

The next witness was Officer Junior, most of whose testimony has already been considered. Levy questioned him at some length about the position of Nan's gloves when he looked into the cab.

Q. Were the gloves folded?

A. No.

Q. How were they?

A. They were laid out straight.

Q. Did they look as though they had been worn, or as though they were laid out straight as indicating that they had not been worn?

MR. RAND: I do not object to the question if the gloves

were brand-new or worn, but as to the purpose for which they had been laid out—

BY THE COURT: Q. So far as the appearance of these gloves enabled you to judge, had they been worn or were they new?

A. They had been worn.

BY MR. LEVY: Q. Did they look as if they had been taken off the hand or were they tight together, smoothed out—you have taken a glove off.

A. Yes, sir, and doubled over once—doubled over lengthwise.

The significance of this testimony will be seen later when Dr. O'Hanlon testifies that he saw no powder and smelled no odor of powder on Nan's hand. The gloves disappeared after Nan's arrest. Could she have fired the pistol with a gloved hand and then removed the glove? If so, is it likely that she would have taken off her gloves, folded them neatly, and placed them upon her knee, beside the face of the man she had just killed? Also, the position and condition of the gloves raise a question as to whether there could have been a struggle just before the shooting.

Junior was the first person to see Nan, just a few minutes after the shooting. His account of her behavior is one of the significant psychological facts in the case. Levy asked him:

Q. What else did the woman say to you on the way to the hospital?

A. She said, "Oh, Caesar, Caesar, what have you done!"

Officer Junior's flat, unemotional rendition of the line was apparently not to the lawyer's liking, and we can be sure that he put all the dramatic fervor he was capable of into it as he repeated his question.

Q. She did not say it that way, did she? "Oh, Caesar, Caesar, what have you done!" She cried out in anguish, didn't she?

A. She was crying.

Q. She cried out as though she were in pain?

A. Well, I don't know as she did. She was crying.

Q. She did not say, "Oh, Caesar, Caesar, what have you done" in that tone of voice, did she?

A. No, sir.

Q. I want you to describe the way in which she said it—did she speak as though she were in pain, as though she were suffering, as though she had had a shock, or did she say it in an ordinary conversational way?

A. She said it as though she was suffering.

Q. Where were her hands while she was doing this or saying this?

A. She was wringing her hands at times.

Q. How many times did she repeat this "Oh, Caesar, Caesar, what have you done," while she was wringing her hands? How many times did she repeat that?

A. A great many times.

Levy had gotten the answers he wanted but he kept hammering away nevertheless on the same theme. Ordinarily this sort of repetition would be poor cross-examination but he knew perfectly well what he was doing. Subliminal suggestion had not yet been invented, but he was planting something that would remain in the background of every juror's mind when they retired to deliberate.

After Junior had testified, Detective Quinn took up the story. The important parts of his testimony have already been told, but his description of the reaction of Julia and Morgan Smith to the news of the tragedy takes on great significance, particularly in the light of the important part they were later to play in the drama.

As soon as the Smiths learned of Nan's arrest they had hurried down to her and arrived breathless at the coroner's court. Detective Quinn was asked:

Q. What took place between the defendant and her sister and brother-in-law when they came in?

A. As soon as J. Morgan Smith and his wife came in—Morgan Smith led the way—and as soon as she saw them she jumped up and she said, "Oh, Morgan, Caesar is dead!" Morgan did not say anything but he stood still like that and the muscles of his jaw contracted as if he was stunned.

Q. What was the color of his face?

A. He turned yellow, almost green.

There can be no doubt that Smith's shock at the news of Young's death was real. If he was part of a conspiracy, as Rand contended, it certainly was not a conspiracy to commit murder.

Captain Sweeney then took the stand and testified to the statement Nan made to him immediately after her arrest. He was followed by William Stemm, Jr., the young man who had heard the shot fired. He testified in part as follows:

Q. Now what was it that first attracted your attention to the cab?

A. The sound of a shot.

Q. Were you facing the cab at the time you heard the sound of a shot?

A. No, sir.

Q. What did you do when you heard the sound of a shot?

A. Looked toward the cab.

Q. What did you notice about the cab at the time you looked into it?

A. Smoke coming out in front of it.

Q. Now, what was the next thing that you saw about the cab that attracted your attention?

A. The cabman lifted the trap and looked into it.

Levy, on cross-examination, tried to get the witness to tell with greater precision the sort of sound he heard.

Q. Now will you describe the kind of sound that you heard?

A. It was muffled and still it was clear. I was excited at the time and could not say.

Q. Now then, that is what I want to get at. You do say it was a muffled report?

A. Muffled and still clear.

Q. You mean a clear muffled report?

A. It was both to me. I could not say which it was. I was excited at the time.

It is understandable that Stemm, who was standing on the sidewalk some distance away, should not have been entirely clear about this. Michaels, the cab driver, who was seated on his perch just above, described it as a loud report. However,

Nan, seated inside the cab, said that she heard a muffled, smothered sound that she thought came from the street. Then she turned around and saw the smoke.

Stemm gave one bit of testimony the importance of which will become apparent later. At the time of the firing of the shot and when the cab arrived at the drugstore, the doors of the cab were open. As they drove off to go to the hospital, the driver closed the doors.

Frederick Michaels, the cab driver, was an unsatisfactory witness. He had been on a tear the night before, and, as he admitted to Mr. Rand, his head was a bit muddled. However, his testimony did contribute additional details to the story.

He said that he heard a "pistol shot" inside the cab, and he described the sound as a "loud report." He was then asked how much time elapsed before Nan opened the trap door and told him to drive to a drugstore. His recollection was tested by the time-honored practice of clapping hands as the lawyers and jurors solemnly gazed at their watches. Michaels' testimony was that Nan opened the trap fifteen seconds after the shot was fired. At the second trial Michaels, after the hand-clapping demonstration, had testified that only seven seconds had elapsed. At any rate, Nan's reaction was almost instantaneous.

Juror Number Three then asked a question about something that must have been puzzling everyone in the courtroom.

By the Third Juror: Q. Would you mind asking the witness why he didn't look into the cab after he heard the shot?

The Court: Answer the question.

A. Why I didn't look in?

Q. Yes.

A. It isn't my place to look in, and another thing, I wouldn't look down. Suppose a shot came from there and I got it?

BY MR. LEVY: Q. You mean you were afraid of being shot?

A. Yes, sir.

I strongly suspect that the cautious Mr. Michaels was not being quite candid and that he knew a lot more than he admitted. It will be recalled that he told the druggist that a man had been shot in his cab, and that Stemm testified that after he heard the shot he saw smoke coming out of it and "the cabman lifted the trap and looked into it."

It is a pity that the cabman was not more honest. He could have thrown much light upon the mystery.

CHAPTER SEVENTEEN

Intercostal Tissues and Dorsal Vertebrae

THE PRELIMINARY EVIDENCE having been completed, the district attorney now proceeded to introduce the most vital proof in the case—the medical testimony. It was his contention that the nature of the wound proved conclusively that Young could not have committed suicide and that if he didn't shoot himself, Nan must have shot him.

Rand called Dr. Edward N. Riggins, the house surgeon at the Hudson Street Hospital. Riggins was a young doctor who had been practicing only a few years. He stated that the dead body of Caesar Young was brought into the hospital at eight-fifty in the morning. The coroner's physician, Dr. O'Hanlon, was immediately summoned, and he performed an autopsy with Dr. Riggins looking on. The cause of death, Riggins said, was "a hemorrhage into the left pleural cavity following a perforating pistol shot wound of the left lung."

Both Rand and Levy had crammed hard for this phase of the trial (it might be mentioned here that in his early days at the bar Mr. Levy had prepared himself for his career by studying anatomy at Bellevue), and from this point on the case became involved in a confusion of medical and anatomical technicalities.

As Rand was about to question Dr. Riggins concerning the course of the bullet, a court attendant carried into the courtroom the upper part of a human skeleton and placed it beside the witness box. Levy was immediately on his feet to protest.

"Permit me to place upon the record my objection to the exhibition of this gruesome object and the use of it at this trial. . . . It is intended to, or will have the effect of, prejudicing or inflaming, perhaps, the minds of the jurors. . . ."

There was a lot more, the point of which was that Levy did not at all like the idea of having this unpleasant reminder of the late Mr. Young in the courtroom throughout the trial. Recorder Goff curtly overruled his objection.

This didn't end the skeleton episode. As Rand started afresh to trace the course of the bullet, Levy got his second wind and also a bright idea. "It is not shown," he objected, "that this is the body of an adult male of the same proportions, size, width, breadth or condition as the skeleton of the deceased or anything approximate to it."

"I think the object is subject to that criticism," said the judge.

Rand protested that one skeleton was pretty much the same as another and that this one was offered merely for illustrative purposes. Levy then temporarily took over the examination and brought out that the doctor could not tell if the bones all came from the same person or whether the skeleton was an assembly of miscellaneous bones—of what Mr. Venus described as "humans warious." Rand insisted that it was like using a map or diagram. After about two hours of wrangling the judge solved the problem by again announcing, "Objection overruled," and the skeleton was marked in evidence.

The case was back once more on the fairway and Dr. Riggins, with the aid of a long needle and a piece of wire, proceeded to show the course of the bullet as it was revealed by the autopsy. "The bullet," said the doctor, "passed through the skin, through the intercostal tissues, through the apex of the left lung and entered the anterior portion of the body at the fourth dorsal vertebra." The bullet, he continued, entered the body "beneath the clavicle, about three quarters of an inch, and to the right of the median line from five to five and a half inches."

Translated into English, this means that the bullet that killed Caesar Young entered his chest just below his left shoulder. It took a downward and rearward course, penetrated the upper part of his left lung, and, after passing through his body, lodged in the spine.

Mr. Levy had been indignant at the production of that "gruesome object," the skeleton. It may be that his pride of showmanship had been piqued at the introduction by his adversary of an exhibit that was sure to be pictured on the front pages of all the newspapers that evening.

Be that as it may, when he arose the following morning to cross-examine Dr. Riggins, the court attendants carried in a life-sized mannequin upon which Mr. Levy and his assistants draped the bloodstained coat and vest that had been worn by the deceased Mr. Young. The newspapers said that Nan paled at the sight.*

In considering this medical testimony it is well to keep in mind that Nan had been seated on the left side of the cab and Young on the right. Mr. Levy spent a considerable part of his cross-examination trying to show that the bullet had gone straight into the body and its course might have been deflected by muscle or tissue. Dr. Riggins gave his opinion that the bullet had entered at an angle of about ninety degrees. "Anything," he said, "may cause deflection."

Q. A handkerchief?
A. Yes.
Q. Skin?
A. Yes, sir.
Q. Tissue?
A. Yes, sir.
Q. Muscle?
A. Yes, sir.
Q. A thread might cause the deflection of a bullet?
A. Possible.

Levy seemed to be making headway but after he had spent a half hour of learned cross-examination on the deflection of

* Years later I was talking to Bayard Veillier about his famous play, *The Trial of Mary Dugan*. "What I know about criminal trials," Veillier said to me, "I learned from your old man. I used to follow him from court to court to hear him try cases. I got the idea of the dummy in *Mary Dugan* from the Nan Patterson case."

bullets, Dr. Riggins gave an answer to one of his questions that apparently settled the matter.

Q. Could you testify under oath, one way or the other, whether that bullet was deflected by the muscle known as the *pectoralis major,* or the muscle known as the *pectoralis minor?*
A. Yes, sir.
Q. Could you say?
A. Yes, sir.
Q. How could you say?
A. The wound was a straight wound through all the tissue.

That question "How could you say?" is an interesting illustration that even the best of lawyers can ask one question too many. The downward, rearward course of the bullet made suicide unlikely unless the bullet had gone straight in and then had been deflected. But if the bullet had gone straight "through all the tissue" it made no difference whether a handkerchief, a thread, or the pectoralis could have deflected it. The fact was, they didn't. The bullet had traveled straight in the direction in which the pistol was pointing.

With the aplomb that all trial lawyers acquire through experience, Levy serenely continued as though he had just received precisely the answer he was looking for. There was a lot more about muscles, tissues, and ribs and then the cross-examiner produced a small bone and handed it to the witness.

Q. I show you this little object and ask you whether it represents a fourth dorsal vertebra?

MR. RAND: May I interrogate the witness on that?

THE COURT: No.

MR. LEVY: Q. I ask you whether that represents a fourth dorsal vertebra?

A. It represents a dorsal vertebra, Mr. Levy, but I cannot say that it is a fourth.

Q. Can you say whether it is the vertebra of a human being?

A. Not surely, no, sir.

Q. Not sure about that?

A. No, sir.

Q. Why can't you tell whether it is the vertebra of a human being or not?

A. It might be the fourth dorsal vertebra of a gorilla.

Mr. Levy produced another bone.

Q. Look at this please, Doctor, and tell me whether you recognize this as being the rib of a human being?

A. It is a rib.

Q. Can you say whether or not it is a rib of a human being?

A. No, sir.

Q. Why?

A. Because I can't.

Q. Can you tell me which rib it is?

A. No, sir.

The dorsal vertebra and the rib were solemnly marked for identification and thenceforth played no part in the trial, but they had served their purpose. The jurors may have been muddled, as I am certain they were, about angles of entry, visceral pleura, parietal pleura, fascia, and other anatomical pleasantries that had been tossed about during the examination, but here was a fact they could thoroughly understand. Here was a doctor, put forward as an expert by the prosecution, who couldn't tell a fourth dorsal vertebra from a sixth, and who didn't know whether a vertebra and a rib were from a man or a gorilla.

Mr. Rand on re-direct asked, "Assuming, Doctor, that the muzzle of this revolver was three feet or less from the point of entrance of the bullet, would any of the substances you named as traversed by that bullet, or all of them, deflect it if fired from a 32-caliber Union Metallic Company cartridge?" To this Dr. Riggins answered, "I do not think there could be deflection."

> Q. But whether it could or not, I understand you to say that in this case there was none. That is right, isn't it?
>
> A. Yes, sir.

Mr. Levy might have left well enough alone, but apparently he remembered something he had forgotten during his main cross-examination, so again he tackled the witness. Have you ever read Professor Ericson's monograph on the deflection of bullets? Or Professor Frank Hastings Hamilton's book on the practice of surgery? Or Professor Ashurst's book as embodied in *The Encyclopedia of Surgery?* Or Professor Guthrie of London, who wrote a book on gunshot wounds?

Dr. Riggins, who was a quite young doctor, confessed that he had never read any of these impressive authorities; in fact he had never heard of most of the authors. So Mr. Levy, who had the books piled up on his table, read extracts to the effect that various substances might easily deflect a bullet, a fact that was not seriously in dispute.

Dr. Riggins had been a candid, intelligent witness, but how much credence could a jury give to a so-called expert who not only could not tell a man's dorsal vertebra from a gorilla's, but who had not even heard of Dr. Guthrie of London?

CHAPTER EIGHTEEN

The Parade of Experts

THE ANCIENT OFFICE of coroner has long since been abolished in New York and has been replaced by a more enlightened system, the County Medical Examiner's office, but in 1904 this hoary anachronism was still flourishing. For many years the office had been filled by political placemen, and it was not unusual, in homicide cases, to have questions of evidence ruled upon and juries instructed in the law by auctioneers, shopkeepers and barbers who were acting in a judicial capacity as a reward for political services.

If I may digress, I remember waiting once in a coroner's court more than three hours for a murder case to be called. It was a freezing cold morning and the coroner, who was a plumber, was out busily repairing frozen pipes that had burst.

Dr. Philip F. O'Hanlon was one of the coroner's physicians and at the time of the Nan Patterson trial he had held that office for about ten years. Whatever were his qualifications as a medical man, and it is my recollection that the coroner's physicians were also appointed as a reward for political activity, there is no doubt that O'Hanlon knew a lot about autopsies.

Rand's direct examination of O'Hanlon, illustrated with the skeleton, needle and wire, was short, and in general it corroborated the testimony given by Dr. Riggins. Then Levy took him over.

Counsel for the defense was interested in how the fatal pistol got into Young's right coat pocket after the shooting, and he ingeniously suggested, by a series of questions, that the deceased might have dropped it into his pocket as the result of reflex action after the shooting. This was possible, of course, if the bullet which entered the spine had not severed the spinal cord, so Levy asked Dr. O'Hanlon about it.

> Q. Taking into consideration, Doctor, the observation that you had of the point of entry of the bullet in that vertebra, would such a wound cause paralysis?
>
> A. Positively no.
>
> Q. So that a person who received such a wound would have full use of his muscles, after the same had been inflicted, for a time?
>
> A. Unless the spinal cord, which is a means of transmitting nerve force, energy, motor and sensory power, was touched, it could not in any way interfere with its motor or sensory power.

Levy then embarked upon a lengthy anatomical examination which was perhaps more intelligible to the jurors who could follow Dr. O'Hanlon's demonstration upon the skeleton than it is to a reader of the stenographic minutes. The doctor admitted that the skeleton was not made up of the bones of one person; in fact, he could not tell if the skeleton was male or female "in the absence of the pelvis."

Then Levy shifted his attack.

Q. Now, Doctor, when you made your autopsy you made your report to the coroner of the city of New York, or the coroner's office?

A. I made my report to Coroner Brown of the city of New York.

Q. The result of your autopsy?

A. Yes, sir.

Q. And the cause of death?

A. Yes, sir, exactly.

Q. Did you report this case as a case of suicide?

MR. RAND: I object to that question as immaterial. The doctor has not given his opinion on it as yet. It is for the jury to say.

THE COURT: I will overrule the objection.

A. I reported this case as a case of suicide.

Q. Now you have had a vast experience in the coroner's office?

A. Yes, sir, but I have not told all that I said about that.

Q. Don't be anxious to volunteer that which is not asked of you.

A. Neither am I anxious to conceal.

Q. Please answer my questions. You reported it as a suicide?

A. No, sir, I did not report it as a suicide.

Q. At that time, based upon your experience extending over many years and thousands of cases that passed through your hands, at that time it was your best judgment that it was a case of suicide, wasn't it?

A. It was my balanced judgment.

Q. But you reported it as a case of suicide, did you not?

A. I don't recall whether I did or not. I had an impression it was suicide.

Q. And that impression was based upon your experience?

A. That impression was based upon experience and deductions.

Q. And the autopsy which you performed?

A. Yes, sir.

The foregoing should be read with interest by students of cross-examination. When Levy made a point—and he had made a good one here—he hung on to it with grim tenacity. It will be observed that he was not only cross-examining, he was summing up all the time. When he finished with this part of the examination it was indelibly impressed on the minds of the jurors that this witness, this veteran of thousands of autopsies, had concluded from what he had seen that Caesar Young had committed suicide.

The cross-examination now turned to another topic.

Q. Speaking about these powder marks, you examined the hand of the deceased, didn't you?

A. I did.

Q. You found powder marks upon his right hand?

A. I found what I believed to be powder marks on the second finger of his right hand.

Q. You have had a good deal of experience with gunshot wounds, haven't you?

A. Yes, sir.

Q. You have seen many persons who have committed suicide or been shot?

A. I have, yes, sir.

Q. You made a microscopic examination of the skin, did you not? What you saw upon the hand of the deceased you believed to be gunpowder marks?

A. I made a microscopic examination of those two black marks, yes, sir.

Q. You believed that they were powder marks?

A. I do believe they were powder marks.

Q. Did you see the defendant at the coroner's office?

A. I did.

Q. The day of the homicide? (Levy slipped here!)

A. I did.

Q. At what time?

A. Prior to my visit to the Hudson Street Hospital.

Q. In the morning, wasn't it?

A. It was around noontime.

Q. Did you examine her hands?

A. I did.

Q. Did you subject her hands to the test of smell?

A. I did.

Q. Besides ocular observation?

A. I did.

Q. Did you smell any powder odor on her hands?

A. I did not.

Q. How do you answer?

A. I did not.

We may be sure that Levy heard the answer the first time, but there was no harm in letting the jury hear it twice.

Q. Did you detect any powder marks upon her hands?

A. I did not.

Q. Positive there were none?

A. I am positive that I did not detect any or there were none there.

Dr. O'Hanlon had been a good witness for the defense and Rand on re-direct did an excellent job in trying to repair the damage that had been done.

First he brought out that although Dr. O'Hanlon had examined Nan's hands he did not examine her gloves. The doctor then said that although in his ten years as coroner's physician he had seen several hundred cases of suicide by gunshot, he had never seen a case in which the pistol was found in the suicide's pocket. This answer was stricken out upon Levy's objection.*

He testified that when he performed the autopsy he knew nothing about the surrounding circumstances. Rand then asked him this:

Q. Was there anything in your knowledge of the case

* In case the layman does not understand the reason for this ruling it should be explained that only evidence relevant to the issues being tried is admissible. What O'Hanlon had seen or not seen in other cases had no bearing upon Nan's guilt or innocence.

other than those one or two black marks on Young's finger to indicate to you suicide?

A. No, sir.

Q. That was the only thing?

A. That was the only thing.

Q. Now I will show you the report to Coroner Brown. I think you are mistaken about that, and if I were inclined to brave the Court's displeasure, I would say that you were too anxious to help Levy. I don't see anything about suicide upon your report. Is that the report you made to Coroner Brown?

A. That is the report.

Q. That doesn't say anything about suicide?

A. Nothing.

Q. You mean that in discussing it orally with Coroner Brown you expressed the opinion you have stated, is that correct?

A. Exactly.

Q. What did you tell the coroner that the direction of the wound indicated?

A. That it was murder.

Dr. O'Hanlon was evidently a man of many opinions. Remember that in answer to one of Levy's questions, he had said that his opinion that it was suicide was based upon the autopsy. Rand attempted to clear up the confusion in a few final questions.

Q. What is your opinion now as to whether or not Caesar Young killed himself?

MR. LEVY: I object to that, sir.

MR. RAND: I have not gone into this question of belief but the defense has.

MR. LEVY: I object to it as incompetent, immaterial and irrelevant. It is for the jury to say. This witness cannot usurp the functions of the jury.

MR. RAND: But if Mr. Levy injects into the case an expression of opinion made by the doctor at an early state of the investigation, it surely must be competent for the district attorney to show what the doctor's belief is now.

THE COURT: You may ask him if he holds that opinion now.

MR. RAND: Q. Do you hold that opinion now—do you hold now the opinion that Caesar Young killed himself?

MR. LEVY: I object to that.

THE COURT: Objection overruled.

A. The opinion I have now is entirely different from the one I had at the original investigation and must be altered by the great amount that has been submitted to me.

Dr. O'Hanlon had wriggled ungracefully out of the predicament he had got himself into, but this much stands out clearly in his testimony: His belated opinion that it was murder was based upon what he had heard and read about the case, but his first judgment that it was suicide was based upon the autopsy and his own observation.

It is pertinent to add here a footnote to Dr. O'Hanlon's testimony. After the case was over, he issued the following statement to the press: "It was not my place to comment on the case before trial, but now that it is over I am free to say that it is my opinion and has been all along that the pistol was in Young's hand when he was shot."

This statement sheds an unflattering light upon Dr. O'Hanlon both as a doctor and as a witness. When he said that it had been his opinion "all along" that the pistol had been in Young's hand when he was shot, the doctor admitted that he had lied under oath in court.

When Dr. O'Hanlon testified Nan Patterson was in the shadow of the electric chair. Yet here is the statement of a professional man and a public official, made after the trial, that might have helped to save her had he made it on the witness stand.

To dispose of this matter of the powder marks, the following day Mr. Rand read the following concession into the record:

> It is conceded by the defense that the pieces of skin from the middle finger of the right hand of Caesar Young, the deceased, containing two black marks testified to yesterday by Dr. O'Hanlon, and taken by him from said finger, were given to Dr. Ernest Lederle of this city for chemical examination as to their substance and composition and that Dr. Lederle's qualifications to make such an examination and to report upon it are unquestioned. It is also conceded that Dr. Lederle testifies that there is no method known to him of chemical analysis by which the composition of these black marks could be ascertained, and further, that he could not determine the composition of these marks by any visual or microscopical examination.

This was a damaging concession and lawyers may wonder why Mr. Levy made it. Dr. Lederle was a man of distinguished reputation and had been a good witness for the prosecution at the second trial. It is my belief that counsel, knowing that the doctor could not be shaken, concluded that the reading of the concession would have a less damaging impact upon the jury than Dr. Lederle's oral testimony on the witness stand would have had.

The next important witness in the procession of experts called by the prosecution was Dr. Charles Phelps, a physician who had been a police surgeon for thirty years. He was an acknowledged authority on guns and pistols and pistol fire and its effects, and had written books on the subject.

Dr. Phelps had made a series of tests which he now described to the jury. Pieces of cloth had been cut from the trousers Caesar Young had worn on the day of his death and the doctor had fired 32-caliber bullets into them at different angles and from different distances. These perforated pieces of cloth, mounted upon a board and labeled, were now exhibited to the jury.

Levy fought desperately, invoking all the rules of evidence in his arsenal, to keep out Dr. Phelps's testimony, but his objections were overruled. The doctor, after comparing the bullet hole in the coat Caesar Young had worn with the pieces of cloth he had experimented with, said that in his opinion the bullet had been fired from left to right, and that the muzzle of the revolver had been held not less than three inches nor more than five from the body.

If the wound in Caesar Young's chest was not a contact wound, this was a body blow to the theory of suicide. A man who is going to shoot himself does not hold the gun from three to five inches away, nor, if he is right-handed, as was later established by Millin's testimony, does he reach over and shoot himself from left to right.

Dr. Phelps then proceeded to explain the basis of his opinion. On the first experimental fragment, which was a contact shot fired point-blank, the hole was large and torn on all sides. The area of burn and blackening was limited and surrounded the hole completely. The contact shot that was fired obliquely showed a hole not quite as large, and the larger part of the burn was on the side from which the shot came.

He then exhibited to the jury pieces of cloth that had been shot from distances of two, three, four, five and six inches, both at point-blank and obliquely. As the distances increased the smudge and the burns were less apparent, and the shots that had been fired obliquely left marks that were almost entirely on the left side. As to the shot fired at a distance of six inches, "it will be noticed," the doctor said, "that there is scarcely any smudge visible."

With intense interest the jurors carefully compared the fragments with the hole in Young's coat. Rand then tried to go into the old question of deflection, but on this he was blocked by his opponent's objections.

When Rand finished his direct examination, Levy announced, "No questions." There were no questions he could have asked Dr. Phelps that would not have made a bad situation worse. A student of the Art of Cross-Examination might give some thought to that equally important art, the Art of Not Cross-Examining.

CHAPTER NINETEEN

The Newsboy's Story

THE PARADE OF EXPERTS was now over and the trial settled down again, not to more important, but to more dramatic and less technical evidence.

Crowley, the cab driver who had driven Nan home from 125th Street in the early hours of June fourth, told how Young had slapped Nan in the face when she refused to get into the cab and had threatened to knock her goddamned head off. Young, the cabman said, was drunk. Another cabbie who had been standing nearby corroborated Crowley.

There was a succession of minor witnesses such as the Smith & Wesson man who identified the pistol as one that had been manufactured by his company.

Levy's cross-examination of George H. Chamberlain, the Smith & Wesson representative, is an illustration of what an astute cross-examiner can do without ammunition. Mr. Chamberlain had testified that the gun that killed Caesar Young had been manufactured by his company in 1898. The Smith & Wesson revolvers were numbered consecutively and this one bore the number 74050. Levy then questioned him:

Q. Let me ask, where are these revolvers made?
A. In Springfield, Massachusetts.
Q. You have a factory in Barcelona?
A. We do not.
Q. Do you know of the existence of a factory there?
A. Yes, sir.
Q. Are there any infringements upon your models made by other manufacturers?
A. There are, yes, sir.
Q. You frequently come across them?
A. We do.
Q. Very frequently revolvers manufactured in infringement upon your models bear the same number as the weapons manufactured by your company?
A. I think not. No, sir. I never had seen any that did.
Q. But they do number those infringed, or rather imitated or copied revolvers, bearing the name Smith & Wesson—they do bear numbers?
A. I am not positive about that. I am not familiar.
Q. Those infringed weapons are made in close imitation of what your company makes?
A. It might be to anybody not familiar with them. It is perfectly easy to anybody familiar with them.
MR. RAND: But they don't bear your name, those infringements?
A. Some of them do in certain ways.
Q. They don't bear the mark of your manufacture? The

infringements are infringements of patents made by other companies in competition with you?

A. No, sir. They are made out of the law.

Q. Illegally?

A. Yes, sir. And they bear our Smith & Wesson mark sometimes.

Chamberlain was not an important witness. He had been called to supply a minor link in the chain the prosecution was forging, but Levy's questions had the effect of injecting an additional element of doubt into the case. There was little question that Young had been shot with the revolver Stern had sold. The proof was virtually conclusive. But supposing some juror believed that the pistol in court might be a forged Smith & Wesson made in Barcelona that by an extraordinary coincidence bore the same numbers as the Stern revolver? It was fantastic, but Rand had the burden of proof and Levy was not missing a chance to insinuate doubts into the case.

Then Rand called Joseph Hewitt to the stand. Hewitt was a boy of about sixteen, a cripple who sold newspapers at Columbus Circle. Under Rand's questioning he said that he knew Nan by sight because she used to buy newspapers from him during the month of May 1904.

He recognized her, he said, because he had seen her picture in the newspapers the day after the shooting, and he remembered that at about eight-thirty on the night of June third he had seen her come out of Pabst's restaurant with a man.

Morgan Smith, who had been brought over to court from the Tombs, was now called up to the railing, where the newsboy positively identified him as the man who had come out of Pabst's with Nan.

They appeared to be quarreling, Hewitt said, and as they walked over to the curb he heard the man exclaim angrily, "You will have to do it!" to which the woman replied, "I won't!" Thereupon the man slapped her in the face and they both got into the cab. Nan seems to have been fated to get slapped a lot that night.

That was all of the conversation that Hewitt heard, but Rand attached great importance to it, and apparently so did Levy, for he put the boy through a stiff cross-examination. Hewitt said that he recognized Smith as the man because he had seen him come out of the St. Paul Hotel two or three times. He admitted, however, that the week before, when Smith was arraigned on the conspiracy indictment, he had been taken to court by a detective from the district attorney's office to see if he could identify him, and he had heard Smith's name called as he stepped up to the bar.

As I have already noted, Rand never made it quite clear what the conspiracy actually was, but it appears implicit in his summing up that he was charging Morgan and Julia Smith with conspiring with Nan to take Young's life. Just how Nan or the Smiths were to profit by that is not evident. In his final address to the jury Rand said:

> If he [Hewitt] did not see Morgan Smith and this defendant in company that night, why doesn't Morgan Smith say so? Is he afraid to pit his word before you against that of this poor newsboy? Here he has been day after day in court. Oh, gentlemen, it is so sickening, it is such rubbish to ask you to suppose that these people were not party to the design to shoot Caesar Young. If there was no conspiracy to take Young fom his wife and keep him with his mistress, if it is not true, do you suppose that all the lawyers in New York could keep Morgan Smith out of that witness chair when you

> think what is at stake here with his own sister-in-law? Oh, can there be but one answer to that question? Morgan Smith dare not contradict Joseph Hewitt. He dare not have you ask him, "What was it Smith said she had to do? What was it she said she would not do?"

Levy's summing up (which, of course, had preceded Rand's) also paid some attention to the Hewitt testimony. The story that the boy had recognized Nan from her newspaper picture was absurd, he said; he called the jury's attention to the unrecognizable pictures that the papers printed at that time. Another, more glaring defect in Hewitt's testimony, he pointed out, was that the undisputed evidence in the case established that Nan had not been in Pabst's that night, but had dined at Healy's several blocks away, and had not left the restaurant until ten o'clock, long after the time when Hewitt said he had seen her with Smith.

"Now what did Smith say to the defendant, if his statement be true," Levy continued, "that can connect that circumstance with the alleged murder of Caesar Young? 'You have got to do it!' Well, do what? Got to dine with him? Got to go to the theater with him? Ride uptown with him? Lend him some money? Possibly that.* And she said, 'I won't!' Does that prove a concerted arrangement? Are they going to spell out of that a preconceived, deliberate purpose to murder?"

I can hardly believe that Hewitt's testimony made much of an impression upon the jury. Even if he was telling the truth

* Levy's slip is rather amusing. He had vigorously fought every effort to prove that the Smiths were constantly broke and were living off the money Young gave Nan. "Possibly that" sounds like an inadvertent admission of the truth of this contention.

about the scrap of conversation he heard, it was such a tiny fragment as to be meaningless.

But the evidence given by the next witness was far from meaningless. The dramatic moment for which the spectators in the crowded courtroom, the press and the entire country had been waiting for almost a year had at last arrived. Rand called Hyman Stern to the stand.

CHAPTER TWENTY

The Nearsightedness of Pawnbroker Stern

UNTIL NOW the third trial had pretty much followed the course of the first two, but after a searching man hunt the pawnbroker and Morgan Smith were about to be brought face to face. There was little doubt in anyone's mind that if Stern identified Smith as the man who had bought the revolver, Nan's doom was sealed.

Mr. Stern was a stout, substantial citizen of evident respectability. He wore glasses with thick lenses, indicating a defective vision that undoubtedly had some bearing upon the accuracy of his observation. The trial had been filled with exciting moments, but there was now a tenseness in the courtroom that surpassed anything that had yet taken place. The pawnbroker stated that he was the owner of a shop at 516 Sixth Avenue, between 30th and 31st streets. This, it might be observed, was a considerable distance from the St. Paul Hotel at 60th Street. Mr. Rand then continued the direct examination:

Q. Did you, on the third day of June 1904, sell this revolver, People's Exhibit 16?

A. Shall I look at the number or anything?

Q. Certainly, look at anything you wish.

A. (*After peering intently at the number of the gun*) Yes, sir.

Q. Do you know at what time of the day you sold it?

A. No, sir.

Q. What time did you get to your place of business in the morning?

A. Generally around nine o'clock; sometimes a trifle later.

Q. Now was the revolver purchased by a person alone or a person in company with another?

A. A person in company with another.

Q. Was the person who purchased the revolver a man or a woman?

A. It was a man and a woman together, sir.

Q. Will you describe, as well as you can, the man as to size; for example, a large or a small man?

A. The man to my recollection was taller than I am, because I remember looking a little up towards him.

Q. Robustly built or otherwise?

A. Well, I should call it robustly—fairly well.

Q. Had he a beard?

A. No, there was no beard on that face that I know of.*

* Persons unaccustomed to testifying in court are inclined to be timid and suspicious of being trapped. I have heard hundreds

Q. As to the woman, do you recall anything about her appearance except that she was smaller than the man?

A. That is about all.

Q. You have already seen this defendant several times, haven't you?

A. At the trial.

Q. Are you prepared to say whether or not this defendant was the woman who accompanied the man who bought the revolver?

A. I cannot say, sir.

Q. One way or the other?

A. No, sir.

Q. You did not pay sufficient attention to it?

A. No, sir.

Morgan and Julia Smith, who were in custody, were now brought up to the railing and they stood there facing the witness.

Q. Will you be good enough to look at Mrs. Smith—it is conceded that she is the lady standing to the left.

MR. LEVY: Yes.

Q. The lady who is brought to the bar. Can you state whether that is the woman who accompanied the man who purchased the pistol?

A. No, sir. I cannot.

THE COURT: One way or the other?

---

of witnesses use this odd, equivocating phrase. Did Stern mean to suggest that the man might have had a beard that he didn't know of?

THE WITNESS: No, sir. I am not certain and I don't remember.

MR. RAND: Will you be good enough to say whether or not in general appearance the person who bought that revolver resembled the man standing at the bar?

MR. LEVY: Objected to.

THE COURT: Objection sustained.

Q. Will you be good enough to say whether in appearance the man who bought this revolver resembled the man before the bar of this court?

MR. LEVY: Objected to.

THE COURT: Objection sustained.

Q. You cannot state definitely whether that is the man or not, can you?

(Objected to. Objection overruled. Exception.)

MR. LEVY: Ask him whether this is the man who bought the pistol.

MR. RAND: I ask him whether he can tell or not, under oath, if that is or is not the man who bought the pistol.

THE COURT: Which man do you refer to?

MR. RAND: The man brought to the bar. Mr. Levy concedes it to be J. Morgan Smith.

THE COURT: What is your answer?

THE WITNESS: No, sir. I cannot.

At this point I will let the reporter from the *Morning Telegraph* describe the scene:

> The dramatic moment of the trial had been reached. "Could you say in a general way the man who bought the pistol resembles the man before you?" asked Rand.

Interest in the courtroom was at white heat. The jurors leaned forward. Smith's features were as rigid as marble and as colorless. An objection from Levy prolonged the suspense. The Recorder sustained the objection. The intake of breath among the auditors was audible.

"Is he the man?" asked Rand, and a hush fell upon the courtroom.

Stern waited—it must have seemed an age to the young woman whose life or liberty was at stake. She sat white-faced like a cornered quarry, shifting her glance from the witness to the jurors.

"Answer!" said the Recorder sharply.

"I cannot say he is the man," said Stern with resolution. Everyone relaxed. Lawyer O'Reilly leaned forward and whispered a word of encouragement to Nan. The color flew to her cheeks. Smith moistened his lips and shifted his weight. But his features were unrelaxed. If Mr. Rand was disappointed he did not show it. The moment that the District Attorney had spent thousands of dollars to bring about was ended.

Q. You won't say?

A. No, sir.

Q. I want to know whether the man who bought the revolver resembled him?

MR. LEVY: Objected to.

THE COURT: Objection sustained.

MR. RAND: Why, Your Honor—

THE COURT: There is no use in arguing the matter. I will not hear argument.

Q. Do you recall the features of the man who bought the revolver?

A. No, sir, I do not.

Q. How old a man should you say from your recollection?

A. Well, it wasn't an old man or a young man. Something around thirty-odd. Something of that sort, I should judge. It may not be quite as old.

Stern further testified that on June 8, 1904, he went down to the district attorney's office and was taken over to the Tombs, where he saw Nan. Later that day he saw her again in the coroner's court. This was only five days after he had sold the revolver. He also said, in response to a question by Levy, that right after June eighth he had been shown some photographs of Morgan Smith.

There are some curious features about Stern's testimony. Rand must have known, or at least anticipated, that he would not identify Smith. Otherwise, why did he try, at the start, to avoid asking the obvious question, "Is this the man who bought the pistol?" Instead he insisted upon asking whether Smith *resembled* the man.

It will be recalled that on June tenth the *Telegram* reported that Stern had been somewhat more explicit in his description of the man who had bought the gun. Smith, it will appear from Julia Smith's testimony, was an occasional customer of Stern's pawnshop and had pawned some of Julia's jewelry there, but Rand did not dare ask Stern if he had ever seen Smith before. If the answer had been "yes," his present inability to identify him as the purchaser of the gun would have been almost conclusive evidence that Smith was not the man.

Frederick Trainor, the clerk at the St. Paul Hotel, corroborated, in general, the story that on the night of June third Nan and the Smiths had gone out to dinner at about seven-thirty and had left word that if Caesar Young called he should say they were at Healy's. They returned to the St. Paul between half-past nine and ten. This was more than an hour after the newsboy, Hewitt, said that he saw Nan come out of Pabst's at the Circle and get into a hansom cab.

The essential parts of the testimony of William Luce, Young's brother-in-law, have already been narrated and need not be repeated, but one interesting circumstance was brought out on Luce's cross-examination. He said that he had known pawnbroker Stern for the past fifteen or twenty years. "When I read in the paper the gun was bought at Stern's," he said, "I went in there after that out of curiosity's sake to ask him if there was any truth in it."

The episode probably had no significance, but it is a strange coincidence that, of all the pawnshops in New York, the lethal weapon should have been bought from an old friend of Young's brother-in-law. (Stern was recalled to the stand later in the trial to testify that Luce had not been in his shop on June third.)

Mr. Rand was building up his case with painstaking care. Julia Smith made a brief appearance on the stand to identify Nan's handwriting to establish a standard of comparison, and then David Carvalho, the famous handwriting expert, was called to say that a letter that had been marked for identification and was later to be put in evidence had been written by Nan.

Flannery, the 125th Street saloon keeper, swore that he remembered the visit of Nan and Caesar to his saloon in the early morning of June fourth. They had about six bottles of ale and stout, he said (no whisky), and some turkey. This provoked Recorder Goff to remark, "It would seem to me to be simply a waste of time to call a witness like that."

The high spots of McKean's testimony have already been told. Officer Quinn was called back to identify the postcard that had been found in Nan's bag, which was then marked in evidence. He could not account for the disappearance of the bag. Nor could anyone at any time thereafter.

CHAPTER TWENTY-ONE

The Beautiful Widow of the Deceased

WHEN MRS. CAESAR YOUNG became a witness at the second trial it was a grim ordeal for Nan. For the first time the defendant and the woman she had so grievously hurt, the mistress and the wife, were brought face to face. The New York *World* described the scene thus:

> The meeting was most dramatic. Miss Patterson was all agitation. She was shaking like a leaf. She appeared to be in deadly fear of the woman whose husband she had stolen. The two women made a decided contrast. Nan Patterson is small and by no means pretty. The widow, on the other hand, is tall and handsome. She appears queenly. She possesses dignity and tact, her voice is sweet, her words well chosen. Few in court yesterday could help wondering why Caesar Young should have left his pretty wife for the *Floradora* actress.

As Rand again called Margaret Young to the stand it was evident that he was playing his trump card. The *World,* we can see from the above description, had lost its heart to the injured widow. It was quite likely that the jurors might do the same.

Mrs. Young briefly recounted her early life with Young. They had been married, she said, on February 18, 1891. Her husband was an owner and breeder of horses and a bookmaker. She managed his property for him and he used to turn over his winnings to her to invest. They lived in Berkeley in a house that they had bought in 1898. Caesar, she said, was a right-handed man.

She did not know Nan, she testified, but she had seen her in California during the winter of 1903–04 at the race track and on ferry boats, presumably with Young, for she said that she had known of the affair since January 1903. From that time she did not cohabit with him until they resumed marital relations when they went to live at the Hotel Walcott in May 1904. This was a subtle point and persuasive of the fact that Young was then on the verge of casting off Nan.

She told of their return to New York from California, Young leaving the train at Chicago, of their brief stay at the Walcott where Young slept every night with her, and then of taking the cottage at Sheepshead Bay.

Q. Now, Mrs. Young, will you describe your husband's manner and appearance during the time of your residence with him at Sheepshead Bay?

A. Well, he was very cheerful and in very good spirits.

Q. As indicated by what actions?

A. He would sing and he would joke and be happy in general.

Then followed an account of the afternoon of June third at the track, the return to New York and the farewell party at the Luces'.

Q. What have you to say about your husband's demeanor and spirits at dinner?

A. He was very, very happy, very lighthearted, kept us all laughing all through the dinner.

Q. What did you hear your husband say down at Sheepshead Bay about his plans for the summer?

A. We planned to go to Scotland, to go fishing and have a good time in general.

Young had relatives in England whom he intended to visit, and also an old friend named Harry Thatcher, who was going to accompany them on the fishing trip in Scotland.

After dinner the men went outside and sat on the stoop and the women remained inside to finish packing the trunks. Young came indoors from time to time, and at about ten o'clock he came in to talk to her about what to put in the trunk for him.

Q. Will you state what he said to you at about half past nine that evening?

A. He wanted me to be sure to put a heavy suit of clothes for him in the steamer trunk. He said, "You know it will be cold on the boat. I just have thin clothes on."

I took the large trunk to get a heavier suit from the bottom, and he was very careful to see that all his wants were properly provided for.

The party broke up at about half past eleven, and Young and Luce left directly together.

Q. Now, when did you next see your husband, Mrs. Young?
A. About twenty minutes of four in the morning.
Q. Where were you when you saw him?
A. I was sitting in the sitting room waiting for him.
Q. And your packing had been—?
A. All completed. Yes, sir.
Q. Now, Mrs. Young, was your husband in the habit of carrying a revolver?
A. No, sir.
Q. Did your husband, himself, have a revolver?
A. He did not.
Q. Did you have one?
A. I did.
Q. (*Handing the witness a revolver*): Is this it?
A. Yes, sir. That is it.
Q. Who gave it to you?
A. Mr. Millin bought it for me when we first moved to Berkeley.
Q. Berkeley is where? In the country?
A. Yes, sir. We lived out in the woods in a remote district.
Q. And your husband was frequently away?

A. Yes, sir.
Q. Did you have that revolver on the third of June?
A. Yes, sir.
Q. Did you pack it?
A. Yes, sir, in my dress suitcase.

The revolver, a Smith & Wesson 38-caliber hammerless, and a box of cartridges were marked in evidence.

Q. Did you ever use any of the cartridges?
A. Yes, sir. I used them one night when I thought there was somebody in the house.
Q. You fired at somebody you thought was a burglar?
A. Yes, sir.
Q. Was this revolver at the time you put it in your suitcase fully loaded?
A. Yes, sir.
Q. Now when your husband came in did you speak to him?
A. Yes, sir.
Q. Was anyone else sitting up with you when your husband came in?
A. Mrs. Luce.
Q. What do you say as to his condition that night regarding the effects of liquor?
A. Well, he was not under the influence of liquor.
Q. Did you go directly to bed?
A. In a few minutes.
Q. Did your husband sleep with you that night?
A. He did.

Q. Did you go directly to sleep or did you talk?

A. Yes, sir. In a very few minutes we went to sleep. He said, "We have to get up early, so don't talk all night."

The following morning Mrs. Young was awakened at five o'clock by the expressman calling for the trunks. The poor woman had had about an hour's sleep. The charge was three dollars and she had no change. Her husband was still asleep.

Q. What steps did you take to get the money?

A. I looked through all his pockets to get the money.

Q. Did you look through all the pockets?

A. Through the trousers and coat and waistcoat.

Q. All the pockets in each?

A. Yes, sir. All the pockets in each.

Q. Was there any weapon of any kind?

A. There was not.

Q. Except a penknife. Was there any revolver in the clothes?

A. There was not.

We cannot fail to be impressed by Mrs. Young's thoroughness. Ordinarily a wife would know where her husband kept his money and would go directly for it—usually in the trousers pocket—and abstract the needed three dollars. But Mrs. Young carefully went through *all* the pockets, in the coat and waistcoat as well as the trousers. Thus we have conclusive proof that Caesar did not have a revolver concealed, not even in one of the small pockets of his vest.

We were struck by Julia Smith's prophetic foresight in looking into Nan's handbag and seeing nothing but a handkerchief there. Now we find that neither Nan nor Caesar packed a concealed weapon and we are left in wonderment how that revolver ever got into the hansom cab.

After the expressman left Mrs. Young went back to bed, but before doing so she took the precaution, tired as she must have been, to count her husband's bankroll—a pleasant connubial touch.

Q. Now where did you take that three dollars from?
A. From his trousers pocket.
Q. Well, was it one of many or not? Was it a large roll of bills?
A. There was a large roll of bills.
Q. Did you count it?
A. Yes, sir.
Q. How much?
A. I know about how much it was. I just went over it quickly.
Q. How much?
A. I got it afterwards and I know exactly how much, Mr. Rand.
Q. We don't suppose you counted it accurately then.
A. There was $1820 in it.

I rather suspect that Mrs. Young, who undoubtedly knew with whom her husband had been the night before, was taking advantage of this opportunity to find out how much he had given Nan.

Q. Now on the morning of June fourth you said you returned to bed with your husband, after the expressman had gone?

A. Yes, sir.

Q. What time did you both get up for the day?

A. Quarter to seven.

Q. You dressed together?

A. Yes, sir.

Q. What time did your husband leave the house?

A. Twenty minutes past seven.

Q. Upon leaving, what did he say? What conversation was there upon his leaving?

Levy objected to this, but the judge allowed the witness to answer as indicating Young's plans and intentions expressed less than two hours before he died.

> MRS. YOUNG: He said he was going downtown to get a shave and buy himself a new hat and would meet me at the pier at nine o'clock and to be sure not to be late. I said, "Don't you be late." He said, "Well, did you ever know me to be late?" I said, "No." He said, "All right."

Mrs. Young also stated that he was going to stop off and buy a new hat because the one he was wearing was battered and he expected that some friends might meet him at Liverpool. The old derby, which had been retrieved from the hat store, was identified by Mrs. Young and marked as an exhibit.

Parenthetically, the uninitiated layman must wonder at the amount of nonsense that sometimes goes into the presentation of a case. The initiated lawyer, or at least this one, also wonders what the solemn admission in evidence of Caesar Young's battered derby was intended to prove.

Rand now turned to the Julia Smith letter that had been one of the most damning bits of evidence against Nan at her previous trial. Mrs. Young said that it had been delivered to her room at the Hotel Walcott at about six o'clock in the afternoon of May third.

Q. Did you open it and read it?
A. Yes, sir.
Q. Did you give it to any person?
A. Yes, sir; I gave it to Mr. Young at about half past seven o'clock, just after we had our dinner.
Q. Did Mr. Young keep it for any length of time?
A. Yes, sir. He kept it overnight and I got it again the next morning.
Q. Did Mr. Young go out that evening?
A. Yes, sir. He remained out until about one o'clock.

Mrs. Young said that before he went out he asked her to write her name on the envelope of the letter and she wrote "Margaret Young."

Rand then offered the letter in evidence, to which Levy objected, and there followed a lengthy legal argument at the conclusion of which Recorder Goff sustained the objection. This was a grievous setback to the prosecution. Justice Davis had admitted it at the previous trial, but the notoriously tough judge upon whom Rand had built such high hopes had failed him in the crisis.

I believe that any lawyer who studies the record will agree

that Goff's ruling was the correct one. "First," he said, "there is no evidence that the defendant authorized the writer of this letter to write the letter. Secondly, there is no evidence that before the letter was written the defendant knew its contents. Thirdly, there is no evidence that after the letter was received that she acknowledged that she knew the contents of the letter at the time it was sent. Fourthly, there is no evidence that she acted upon the matter contained in the letter. I therefore sustain the objection."

The effect of Goff's ruling was realized by the press. The New York *Express* declared in a three-column headline:

HARD BLOW TO PROSECUTOR OF NAN WHEN "JULIA" LETTER IS RULED OUT

The *Express* article stated:

> What is regarded as the worst blow the prosecution in the Nan Patterson case has received was delivered yesterday when Recorder Goff ruled out the letter written by Mrs. J. Morgan Smith to Caesar Young a month before the murder and which formed the basis of the conspiracy charge against the actress as well as against her sister and brother-in-law. The letter had been regarded by Assistant District Attorney Rand as the foundation of the charge of murder in the first degree against the former actress, and his disappointment was apparent when the Recorder refused to admit the missive in evidence.

With the exclusion of the letter Mrs. Young's testimony ended. Mr. Levy very sensibly announced that he had no questions to ask her. It is an elementary rule of cross-examination that women and children should be handled with delicacy.

Bereaved widows, especially those whose husbands have been eliminated by violence, should be avoided like the plague. The tragic presence of the lovely Mrs. Young must have prejudiced the twelve chivalrous jurors immeasurably against Nan, and her lawyer was wise to get the widow off the witness stand as quickly as possible.

CHAPTER TWENTY-TWO

Caesar's Mistress Must Be above Suspicion

ALTHOUGH RAND was unsuccessful in getting the "Julia" letter in evidence he did succeed in getting in, over Levy's vigorous objection, another letter that may have done Nan considerable harm. This was a letter written to Young's friend Leslie Coggins, the man who had told Julia that Young did not intend to marry Nan. The letter was signed "Cry Baby," but the handwriting expert David Carvalho had identified it as being in Nan's handwriting.

During her stay in California Nan had been in a hospital for a slight operation and the letter had been written from there. Parts of the letter follow:

DEAREST:

Was afraid you had forgotten all about your little girl. I am feeling fine and dandy tonight, sweetheart. Have been up all day long. I am going home tomorrow about two o'clock. What do you think of that? Isn't that great? Gee, hon, I'm so glad I can't wait for morning to come.

Y. is coming up in the morning, I think. He was here all this morning. I'll bet I have more to tell you than you have me. Will ring you up from my room tomorrow night if you will send me another note tonight to say where you will be at a certain time. I am going to give a party to a few of the nurses who have been more than good to me, and I wish you could run up for a minute later on, but maybe it will be better until I leave this —— place. What do you think, dear?

Just send me a real long note because they do help to cheer me up. Please send this back in your note, hon, as I really think it best. Be a good boy and do as mother says. All my love and kisses.

CRY BABY

If you should walk on the other side of the street I would see you from my little window, but don't say I told you.

C.B.

There was no date and since Rand was blocked in his effort to prove when Nan was in the hospital he was unable to show when the letter was written. The purpose of introducing the letter was to demonstrate that in spite of Nan's protestations of devotion to Young she was having a love affair with another man and writing him love letters.

Levy contended that the letter might have been written before Nan had become intimate with Young, but the internal evidence shows that he was wrong. The initial Y undoubtedly refers to Young in spite of counsel's ingenious suggestion that lots of men have that initial. And Nan's concern about having her note returned certainly is an indication that she was double-crossing her lover.

Rand, in his summing up, used the Coggins letter most effectively. After reading it again to the jury he said, "Now if there was any doubt left whatever that this is a love letter of a kept woman making an assignation with a friend of her keeper, it is supplied in this sentence, 'Please send this back in your note, honey, as I really think it best.' Why should she want her note returned unless she knew that it was evidence of her disloyalty to Young?"

CHAPTER TWENTY-THREE

Julia Smith Takes the Stand

THE CASE for the State was now almost all in, but there was yet one more important witness to be called. It is my impression that Rand was reluctant to call Julia Smith but that he felt obliged to do so because of Goff's exclusion of her letter.

Julia Smith appears to have been an alert, intelligent woman and more attractive than her sister. The *Evening Journal* described her thus:

> Mrs. Smith is very much like her actress sister in manner, there is a strong physical resemblance between them. She is slender, however, while Nan is rather stout. She has heavy black hair in which the threads of gray have crept prematurely. Her eyes are snappy and expressive. She is perfectly self-possessed under the most trying circumstances. She is scrupulously neat and wears with taste the few articles of apparel left to her after her wanderings of last summer, fall and winter. She is careful of her speech without seeming to be so, and her utterances are never hasty or ill-considered.

Mrs. Smith was called to the stand by the prosecution as "a hostile witness." This phrase has a technical meaning to lawyers. Ordinarily, in a trial, the lawyer who calls a witness is said to vouch for his credibility and is restricted in his examination by certain rules. He may not lead the witness and he may not impeach the witness's credibility. There are times, of course, when such limitations would be unfair and unreasonable. A lawyer occasionally has to call an obviously antagonistic witness. In such a case the judge may, in his discretion, permit the examining lawyer to treat the witness as "a hostile witness" and examine him as if he had been called by his adversary. This was the situation with Julia Smith.

Mrs. Smith's testimony was the longest in the entire trial; it covers one hundred and thirty-four pages in the typewritten minutes. However, much of the time she was on the stand was taken up by legal controversy between the lawyers.

I have already presented portions of her testimony. She first met Young, she said, when she visited Nan in California in the spring of 1903. She knew, of course, of the relationship that existed between Young and her sister and he told her a number of times that he was going to marry Nan as soon as his wife consented to a divorce.

She became quite friendly with Young after her return East and they corresponded frequently. Unfortunately she destroyed all his letters.

"You called him 'Nunc'?" Rand asked.

"I did."

" 'Nunc' was an endearing term for 'uncle,' wasn't it?"

"I called Mr. Young 'Nunc' to please him because he did not want me to call him Mr. Young, and I did not like to call him Caesar."

"To all intents and purposes he was married to your sister, wasn't he?"

"He was."

"And you were practically his extra-legal sister-in-law?"

"I suppose that is what you would call it."

"His morganatic sister-in-law," Levy interjected.

Julia then told of Nan's return to New York, of her agitation at hearing what Coggins had said, of writing the letter to Young, and of Nan's apparent reconciliation with Young that night.

Rand then made another desperate effort to get the letter in evidence but Goff stuck to his ruling. This was a vital matter to the prosecution, so the assistant district attorney persisted in his questions.

> Q. Did you write this letter in a state of feeling brought on, or increased, if you choose, by the conversation you had with your sister Nan that day?
>
> A. My feeling was increased by my conversation with my sister. Yes, sir.
>
> Q. Did you write this letter?
>
> A. I did write the letter.
>
> Q. Did that letter truthfully represent your feelings?
>
> A. Yes.
>
> MR. RAND: Now I again offer the letter in evidence . . .
>
> THE COURT: Objection sustained.

Rand had failed to achieve his main purpose in calling Julia Smith as a witness. The letter was out and stayed out, so, for the time being, he accepted the ruling of the court and turned to another matter—the date of the Coggins letter. If he could prove conclusively that at the time Nan was Young's mistress she was carrying on a clandestine love affair with another man, it would do much to strip her relationship with Young of the romantic glamour with which the defense was trying to invest it and show Nan up as a mercenary, meretricious creature.

Julia readily admitted that Nan had been in the hospital for an operation around Christmas time in 1903. That seemed to settle the matter. Rand had scored an important point, but only momentarily. Then Julia, who was demonstrating admirably that she was a resourceful and quick-witted witness, remembered that Nan had also been in the hospital a year earlier, around the time she first became intimate with Young.

A few more questions concluded the direct examination and Levy arose to cross-examine the witness. As he proceeded to bring out the events immediately preceding the tragedy, he was sharply reminded that this was not cross-examination.

"This is new matter not touched upon by the prosecution," Goff said. "You are making this witness your own and you must be limited under such rules as are applicable to her examination."

"Your Honor means that I cannot lead the witness? I do not intend to," Levy replied. From this point on Julia Smith was technically a defense witness.

The lawyer took her through the events of June third and June fourth—the visit to the track, the return to the St. Paul, dinner at Healy's, the telephone calls, and Nan's departure that night. She returned at about four in the morning, Julia said. "She was quiet and normal. She did not seem particularly happy, but she was not agitated." Levy finished his examination with the occurrences of the following morning, including Julia's fortunate inspection of the contents of Nan's handbag.

Rand was now in a position to put Julia through a stiff grilling, which he proceeded to do. His first target of attack was the disappearance and unexplained absence of the Smiths for almost a year.

"You say you were in New York on June eighth?" he asked. This was the day before the Smiths vanished.

The Recorder overruled Levy's objection, but Julia had been prepared for the question.

"No," she answered. "Mr. Rand, I would like to answer questions about things that happened after the fourth of June, but I am under indictment, as you know, and my counsel has advised me not to answer questions, because any answers I may make may tend to degrade, incriminate, or subject me to a penalty."

Rand was expecting the answer and was ready for it. He now pulled a clever grandstand play.

"I think I can cover that," he said. "I am, for the present, the district attorney of this county. I state to you that if you will now answer my questions I will, on Monday morning, go before His Honor, the judge presiding in Part I, whoever he may be, and will move to have the indictment now pending against you dismissed with a great deal of pleasure. Now will you answer my questions?"

Julia replied that she could not answer any questions until she first consulted her lawyer, so the court took a recess for that purpose. When she returned to the stand, Rand continued his questions and she continued to refuse to answer. Then Recorder Goff took a hand.

"Madam, I will ask you this question. The district attorney says that he may dismiss the indictment pending against you. If he should do so would that affect your reason for refusing to answer this question?"

Mr. Levy: Note my objection to Your Honor's question.
The Court: Do you understand the question? If the district attorney should dismiss the indictment pending against you, would the dismissal of such indictment affect the reason which you have given for refusing to answer the question?
Mr. Levy: I object to Your Honor's question as immaterial and improper, and on the further ground, if Your Honor please, that these negotiations cannot be made the subject matter of interrogation of the witness before this jury.
Mr. Rand: Would that affect your reason?
A. No, sir, because my answers may degrade me.

Then the examination continued in this fashion:

Q. Did you leave New York on the eighth of June?
(Objection; objection sustained.)
Q. Did you and your husband leave New York?
(Objection; objection sustained.)
Q. Did you on the evening of June eighth register under an assumed name at Meyer's Hotel, Hoboken?
(Objection; objection sustained.)
Q. Did your husband then go to Washington?
Mr. Levy: I object to that as incompetent. I ask Your

Honor to admonish the district attorney not to proceed with this line of interrogation.

THE COURT: I do so.

Rand argued vigorously but Goff was not one to change a ruling once he had made it. The assistant district attorney was blocked in his attempt to prove directly the wanderings of the Smiths, so he tried another tack. This time he was somewhat more successful.

Q. Did you ever see Hyman Stern?
A. In court here.
Q. Did you ever see him anywhere but in court?
A. No, sir.
Q. Did you ever see him in Toronto?
A. No, sir.
Q. Did you know he was in Toronto this year?

Levy objected to this and the succeeding questions, but his objections were all overruled.

Q. In March of this year did you know he was in Toronto?
A. Of my personal knowledge, no.
Q. You heard he was, didn't you? I didn't ask you about personal knowledge.
A. I was told so by a detective afterward.
Q. Wasn't it on the thirteenth of March you heard he was there?
A. I really couldn't say. It was in March.
Q. Was your husband living with you then in Toronto?
A. He was.

Q. Did he go to some other place? Did he start on a journey in March?

Another legal argument ensued in which Levy was learnedly backed up by his partner, Henry Unger. Then the prosecutor reframed his question.

Q. After you had learned that Stern was in Toronto this March, didn't you and your husband leave Toronto?

A. I refuse to answer because any answers I may make may tend to degrade or incriminate me.

Rand now made another futile attempt to introduce Julia's letter to Young in evidence. His persistence indicates the importance he attached to it, but the Recorder adhered to his ruling and refused to admit it.

Then Rand had another letter marked for identification. This letter has not survived but the lengthy argument that followed gives a clue to its contents. It was apparently written in Cincinnati on March 29, the night of her arrest, by Julia to her sister Nan in the Tombs.

In arguing for its admission Rand said, "The effect of these statements is that the Morgan Smiths had been in the city of Toronto; that they knew that Stern, the pawnbroker, had gone there for the purpose of identifying them, and that as soon as he came to Toronto they fled from Toronto, and that they had information that Stern was to be sent again as soon as they could be located in other places where Stern could identify them. I think certainly, as far as my judgment is concerned, that that is tantamount to an admission that they were concerned in the purchase of this revolver. I don't say it is an express admission."

It is surprising that this argument should have been permitted in the presence of the jury. Goff did not allow the letter in evidence, but the jurors must have had some idea of what Julia had written to her sister. Stern's name had not been mentioned, but in the letter there were references to someone called "S."

"Who is the 'S' referred to there?" Rand asked.

"I must decline to answer," Julia replied, "because any answers I may make may tend to degrade or incriminate me."

Rand pounded away at the question with all the vigor he was capable of but the witness stubbornly continued to invoke her constitutional privilege.

> Q. Now I want to ask you, madam, is it your honest belief that to tell this jury what you meant by *S* in quotation marks in this letter would tend to degrade or incriminate you?
>
> A. I must decline to answer.
>
> Q. Now, madam, I state to you again that if you will answer my questions I will never prosecute you.*
>
> MR. LEVY: I object to this statement being made to the witness.
>
> THE COURT: I sustain the objection.

Julia stuck to her guns and was not compelled to answer the

* It may be stated here that the Smiths never were prosecuted. Some time after the Nan Patterson case ended the district attorney moved to dismiss the indictment against them. It is clear that Rand never intended to try their case. The indictment was solely a device to bring them into the jurisdiction and keep them locked up during Nan's trial.

question. Rand then offered the letter in evidence and the court refused to admit it.

Rand was beginning to lose his temper. "Your Honor will permit me to ask no questions," he exclaimed, "about statements made by this witness, in effect admissions that they bought the revolver."

This was a highly improper statement. There was no such admission and the letter was not before the jury. Levy immediately protested. "I ask Your Honor to admonish the jury that there is no such evidence in this case."

"I so admonish them," said the judge.

Rand then produced another letter which he now offered in evidence and which the court excluded. However, it found its way into the daily newspapers—I dislike to think with the connivance of the district attorney. It was written by Julia Smith while she was at home in Washington, D. C. It was dated July 9, 1904, and was addressed to her husband, who, under the name of W. A. Adams, was staying at St. Lawrence Hall in Montreal. Here is part of the letter:

> *Dear God, why do I argue? Isn't it your safety I am thinking of? Isn't it better than in New York behind the bars? Aren't they after you now as much as ever? . . . My staying here at home was for the purpose of reducing our expenses to a minimum thus relieving you of that at least. You are to stay under cover as much as possible until the trial. I don't know yet if they will use you as a witness or not. I should think they would have to, but in this case I am not trusting to my own judgment but am simply acting under orders as you are.*

Judge Goff had refused to permit the jurors to see this letter but we can be pretty sure they all read it the following morning at breakfast before leaving for court.

The defense had been successful, so far as the judge's rulings were concerned, but Rand's unanswered questions and Julia's repeated statement that her answers might tend to incriminate or degrade her must have hurt the defendant's case seriously.

CHAPTER TWENTY-FOUR

The Drama of the Pawn Tickets

Now occurred a regrettable episode. It may have been that Rand's frustration at the rejection of his most important evidence caused him here to overstep the bounds of proper advocacy. At any rate, he now attempted a trick that was not only inexcusable but curiously clumsy for a lawyer of his skill and experience.

After several questions, to which the court sustained objections, that indicated that Morgan Smith had been in serious financial straits around the time of the shooting, Rand produced several pieces of jewelry—two bracelets and a ring—which he showed to the witness. Julia identified the articles as hers. She didn't remember when she had seen them last but she was sure she had not seen them since the fourth of June.

Rand then produced several pawn tickets, which he held in his hand as he proceeded with his cross-examination.

Q. Did you know that these articles were pawned?
A. I did.
Q. You cannot tell this jury whether you ever saw these tickets before?
A. I cannot.
Q. Who pawned them for you, do you know?
A. My husband.
Q. Did he tell you where he pawned them?
A. He did not.
Q. Don't you know that People's Exhibit 51, People's Exhibit 52, and People's Exhibit 53 [the jewelry] were pawned by your husband, J. Morgan Smith, with a pawnbroker named Hyman Stern on the third day of June, 1904?
A. I do not know, Mr. Rand, with whom they were pawned.

The atmosphere in the courtroom was suddenly charged with electricity. Rand was a lawyer of the highest standing at the bar, and surely no lawyer of repute would ask a question like that unless he had evidence to back it up. If Rand could prove that Morgan Smith had been in Stern's pawnshop on the day the pistol was bought, it would be convincing evidence that he had been the purchaser. As he continued his questions Rand waved the tickets before the witness.

Q. Don't you know that Exhibits 54 and 55 are the pawn tickets for these articles pawned at the pawnshop of Hyman Stern?

A. You have just shown them to me.

Q. You do not need to see them again.

A. I did not look at the dates of them at all.

Q. Will you confine yourself to answering my questions?

A. I will.

It should be noted that although Rand referred to the tickets as exhibits he had not offered them in evidence; they had merely been marked for identification.

Q. The question is whether or not you do not know that these tickets, People's Exhibits 54 and 55, are the pawn tickets calling for these articles pledged at the pawnshop of Hyman Stern?

MR. LEVY: If they are of June third we will consent that they shall go in evidence.

THE WITNESS: They are October—

MR. RAND: Pardon me. Didn't you promise me that you would answer my questions?

THE WITNESS: I beg your pardon. I did not mean anything wrong.

The New York *Herald* reported that Julia smiled in triumph and Mr. Levy was heard to chuckle audibly. The witness, with a quick glance, had seen the dates on the tickets, so Rand now had to modify the question he had previously asked. He no longer referred to the jewelry as having been *pawned* on June third.

Q. Don't you know that these tickets bearing the dates they do—look at them—

A. I have looked at them.

Q. —are renewal tickets of articles pawned on the third day of June 1904?

MR. LEVY: The purpose of my friend is to create an impression that is not sustained by the evidence.

MR. RAND: May I ask counsel to state his objection?

THE COURT: I will not hear argument, Mr. Levy.

MR. LEVY: I object unless the dates upon the tickets are disclosed to the jury.

THE COURT: I overrule your objection.

Q. Will you answer the question. Don't you know these two tickets, Exhibits 53 and 54, are renewal tickets of articles pawned by J. Morgan Smith at the pawnshop of Hyman Stern on the third day of June 1904?

A. No. I have no real knowledge of these tickets.

An offer of the tickets in evidence would have settled the matter but Rand still did not offer them. Instead he abruptly shifted his line of questioning to Hyman Stern's visit to Toronto. His purpose was obvious. If the jewelry had actually been pawned on June third, Morgan Smith had a good reason for avoiding the pawnbroker in Canada.

Q. Mrs. Smith, were you in Toronto in March 1905?

A. I refuse to answer, Mr. Rand.

Q. Was it in Toronto that you learned, as you stated this morning, from a detective, that Hyman Stern had been in Toronto?

A. I must refuse to answer that question, Mr. Rand.

Q. Didn't you leave Toronto because you did not want Stern to see yourself and your husband?

A. I refuse to answer.

Q. Did not your husband leave a barbershop in Toronto where he was being shaved without having the shave completed when Hyman Stern entered it in March 1905?

Levy's objection to this question was sustained.

Q. I suppose you did not go with your husband to barbershops.
A. Hardly.
Q. You were perfectly willing to have Stern see you at any time?
A. I certainly was.
Q. Had you reason to suppose that any harm could come to you from Stern's seeing you?
A. I had no reason to think that Stern could harm me in any way.
Q. Had you any reason for avoiding Stern?
A. No.
Q. Had you any reason for leaving Toronto on the day Stern appeared there?
A. I must refuse to answer, Mr. Rand.
Q. Why?
A. Because it may tend to degrade or incriminate me.
MR. RAND: That is all.

That concluded Julia Smith's testimony, and Rand still had not offered the pawn tickets in evidence. If he was bluffing, it was a dangerous bluff and, it seems to me, a foolish one. Juries are resentful of a lawyer intimating that he has certain evidence if he does not follow it up with proof. But if it was a bluff, Levy was quick to call it. When Rand announced that he was through with the witness his opponent arose.

> Mr. Levy: I call for the production of those pawn tickets, marked for identification.
>
> Mr. Rand: No. When they are admitted in evidence they may be shown, but I decline to show counsel for the defense—
>
> Mr. Levy: I ask that they be marked in evidence.
>
> Mr. Rand: I will consent to that. Please mark them.
>
> Mr. Levy: I desire to offer them in evidence but before doing so I would like to look at them.
>
> Mr. Rand: Not until they are marked in evidence. Then I will gladly show them.
>
> Mr. Levy: They were shown to the witness.
>
> The Court: Is it your purpose to offer these tickets in evidence without regard to what they may disclose by your examination?
>
> Mr. Levy: Yes.
>
> The Court: Show them to Mr. Levy. They are to be marked in evidence without any further motion or argument. Show them to Mr. Levy and then mark them in evidence.

The pawn tickets were marked as exhibits. Rand's bluff had been called.

"I will read them to the jury," Levy said.

"I should read them if anyone," Rand protested. "I have offered them and he has consented and they have been marked in evidence on my cross-examination."

Rand realized the damage he had sustained and he was

making an effort to repair it by trying to get credit for putting the tickets into the record. It took considerable audacity for him to say coolly, "I offered them," in the presence of the jurors who, a few minutes before, had heard his opponent offer them.

The pawn tickets were read to the jury. They showed that Julia Smith's bracelets and ring had been pawned with Hyman Stern on October 7, 1904.* Incidentally, the ring had been pledged for five dollars. The Smiths must have been pretty hard up.

I fancy that Rand regretted that he had brought the whole matter up, but Levy was not yet satisfied and fired a devastating parting shot.

"I call upon the district attorney," he said, "to produce the pawn tickets bearing the date June 3, 1904, so that I may offer them in evidence."

"The district attorney hasn't got them," Mr. Rand replied.

"That is all, Mrs. Smith," said Mr. Levy.

The episode of the pawn tickets was a sorry affair and, as a lawyer, I wish Rand had not done what he did. Aside from its questionable ethical propriety, it was a reckless gamble that had little chance of succeeding with an adversary as astute as Levy was. Rand's attempted explanation, as I shall point out in a moment, was implausible, and I am sure that the entire affair worked greatly to the defendant's advantage.

* There is something puzzling here. In October 1904 the Smiths were wandering about the country. It is hard to understand how he could have pawned the jewelry at Stern's on that date unless he had temporarily returned to New York, which seems hardly likely. If he had, it is highly improbable that he would have gone to the one pawnshop in the city where he was most certain to be recognized.

Levy, in his summing up to the jury later on, was to use the pawn tickets with telling effect:

"I shall have occasion throughout my argument," he said, "to point out to you evidence of the unfair insinuations into this case—not of evidence of sworn witnesses, but rather ideas and suggestions which the district attorney himself has evolved so as to delude and deceive you twelve gentlemen into the belief that there is evidence bearing upon these propositions.

"Not alone should he be fair with this defenseless girl here, but he should be fair in his dealings with you twelve men who are not lawyers, who have the right to lean upon him, not for misguidance but for guidance.

"Let me point out the pawn-ticket episode, to the pawn tickets which he wanted to delude you into believing bore the date of June 3, 1904. He knew that the evidence was incompetent, and if the tickets were ruled out of evidence you could not see them.

"He takes a fragile, defenseless, weak woman whose condition approached close to hysteria at the moment he says to her, holding out the tickets, 'Did you pawn those articles on June third? Were those articles pawned on June third?' 'Let me see the tickets,' said the woman. 'Why, Mr. Rand, these tickets are dated in October,' and then he refused to show me the tickets.

"It was only after I promised the learned judge that I, myself, would put them in evidence that the tickets were shown to me and I did put them in evidence. They were incompetent as bearing upon this girl's guilt or innocence, but I offered them so as to have a perfect lesson spread before you, gentlemen of the jury, of the unfair methods and tactics of the learned gentleman opposed to me.

"He attempts to deceive you by giving you the impression that June third was the date of these tickets, and mark you, gentlemen of the jury, if I had not interposed those tickets in evidence myself, you could not have any impression other than they were dated June third.

"They called Stern, the pawnbroker. Why didn't they call Stern's clerk? They called Stern, the pawnbroker. Why didn't they produce Stern's books? They called Stern, the pawnbroker. Why didn't they bring the books which the law requires every pawnbroker to keep, to show whether or not on the third day of June there was a pistol sold; to show whether on the third day of June 1904, as was insinuated, there were any articles of jewelry pawned; to show whether these pieces of jewelry were ever pawned at Stern's place?"

Rand had fallen into his own pit. It is an interesting study in advocacy to see how, in his summation, he tried to climb out of it. In his final address to the jury he devoted quite a bit of time to the pawn tickets. There is too much of it to quote in its entirety, but the gist of his argument was that he had been anxious to put the tickets in evidence, but he knew that they were inadmissible, so he laid a carefully prepared trap for his opponent, who innocently allowed himself to be caught in it.

It is worth while to remind the reader again that Rand had ended his examination of Julia Smith without even making an offer to put the tickets in evidence. Here is part of what Rand said:

"What are the facts? Mrs. Smith, a sister of this defendant, was on the stand. I wanted to put in evidence before you, as I told you at the time, two pawn tickets from the pawnshop of Hyman Stern for the purpose of showing you that the Smiths were regular customers of Hyman Stern and were in the habit of pawning their personal trinkets there. That purpose I stated to you. I disclaimed at once the suggestion that I wanted you to believe that the articles were pawned on the third of June or that these tickets were dated June third. . . .

"All right. Well, the tickets bear the dates October 5, 1904, and October 20, 1904. When I put them in evidence they would at once show to you that the dates were in October 1904 and not in June 1904, and would therefore defeat the very object which he says I was trying to accomplish. Now wouldn't I have been an ass, a fool, a muddle-headed fool, and that is about the only thing I wasn't called yesterday.

"Now I did ask a question of the witness, 'Don't you know that these are renewal tickets for articles pawned on the third of June?' and I will tell you why I asked it. The witness on the stand was the defendant's sister. I was absolutely fair to her. It does not follow that to be fair to her I have to allow her to juggle with me and fool you. . . .

"Now when I asked that question do you remember what occurred long before Julia Smith read the face of the pawn ticket? Levy was up in the air. Now I had not shown him the tickets. I had been careful to keep them in my pocket all that afternoon. Levy was up in the air shouting, 'Those tickets are not dated in June. Those tickets are dated in October.' I wonder how he knew. I wonder how he knew. He had not gotten that information from me. Well, of course, that spoiled the cross-examination, as it was intended to, for the time being. He gave the tip to the witness that she needed. . . ."

(If the reader will turn back to the testimony, which has been accurately quoted above, it will be seen that Rand's statements bear a very slight resemblance to what had occurred. But the district attorney always has the last word. The defense had no opportunity to reply.)

"The minute she got them in her hand, she said what Levy wanted her to say. She said, 'Why, Mr. Rand, those tickets are dated in October.' You see I did want those tickets in evidence and I did have some difficulty in getting them in . . . Now I haven't practiced law long compared with my experienced opponent. I am a novice in this sort of thing, and I thought perhaps he would help me. I thought perhaps that what I could not do alone Levy and I could do together and I knew how willing he would be to help me . . ."

So Mr. Levy naïvely fell into the trap that his crafty opponent had prepared for him, and offered the pawn tickets in evidence. Mr. Rand, it will be seen, did not mention that there was nothing on the tickets to show that they were renewals, nor does he mention that there was absolutely no proof that Morgan Smith had pawned anything on June 3, 1904.

CHAPTER TWENTY-FIVE

End of the Testimony

As at the previous trial, the final witness for the prosecution was the widow of the deceased, Margaret Young. There was nothing she could add to the evidence already given, but, as I have already pointed out, it was an effective, dramatic finish.

Rand asked if her husband had ever asked her to consent to a divorce. Levy's objection was sustained. Rand then asked her, "Did you and Mr. Young have any children?"

"No."

"At no time?"

"No."

The childless widow left the stand and Mr. Rand in a loud voice—the *Herald* said "shout"—announced, "The People rest!"

It was late Friday afternoon and Mr. Levy was asked by the court if he intended to put in any defense. He said that he had not yet made up his mind, so the court, with the understanding that he would advise Mr. Rand of his intentions by ten o'clock that night, took a recess until Monday morning.

The entire battery of defense counsel now repaired to the Tombs, where they were joined by Nan. It was an important decision to make although I fancy it had been made long before the conference.

Perhaps the most important decision a criminal lawyer ever has to make is whether or not to put his client on the stand. The judge has to charge the jury that a defendant does not have to testify, and that no presumption arises from a defendant's refusal to become a witness.

Nevertheless it is difficult for jurors to follow this admonition. They have listened to the prosecution's witnesses and it is natural for them to want to hear the defendant's version. In this case it must have been particularly difficult. All the evidence had been circumstantial. Nan and Caesar had been the only persons in the cab, and Caesar was dead. I can imagine most intelligent jurors asking, "Why doesn't the only living person who knows what happened tell us about it?"

It was a hard decision to make—to keep Nan off the stand and put in no defense—but that is what her lawyers decided. She had been an excellent witness at the second trial, but she had been through a grueling ordeal for a year, her nerves must have been on edge, and it would have been risky to try her luck a second time.

There was, possibly, another good reason for not letting her testify. When the Smiths were arrested in Cincinnati the detectives had seized a number of letters, some of them presumably from Nan to her sister. The defense lawyers made a motion before Mr. Justice William J. Gaynor for their return and the prosecution was ordered to give them back. But we can be sure that the prosecution first read them, and they probably contained statements that could have been used on Nan's cross-examination with damaging effect.

Mr. Levy notified the district attorney that night that when court convened on Monday morning the defense would rest its case. The evidence was all in. Nothing remained now but the oratory and the verdict.

CHAPTER TWENTY-SIX

The Defense Sums Up

UP TO NOW the battle, bitter though it had been, had been fought with a reasonable regard for the professional amenities. But the major participants had been in the case for almost a year and their nerves were frayed and their tempers acerbated. As the two lawyers faced each other for the last round the gloves were off and no holds were barred. Rarely in legal history have two advocates of stature and experience attacked each other with such savage intensity.

Popular excitement had been mounting and it now surpassed anything that had yet occurred. Said the New York *Times:*

> The closing scenes of the trial are arousing public interest to a degree almost unprecedented in the history of criminal cases in New York. An hour before the doors were opened yesterday morning the court building was besieged by a throng which numbered thousands. Some of those who

> sought admission said they were relatives of President Roosevelt, of Police Commissioner McAdoo, of Mayor McClellan and other distinguished men. Even those who were connected with the case had difficulty getting in.

The newspapers reported that Mrs. Rand, who had come down to court to hear the speeches, was refused admittance and it was not until a half dozen assistant district attorneys came to her rescue that she was finally permitted to enter the courtroom.

Mrs. Levy also had an experience that has become a familiar legend in the family. She was determined to hear the final speeches, so she went to Mr. Levy's office and one of his young assistants took her to the courthouse. They managed to struggle to the door of the courtroom but there they were stopped by the officer in charge. "But this is Mrs. Levy," her escort protested. "Sorry," said the court officer. "I've already let in three Mrs. Levys and I ain't going to let in any more of them." Somehow she convinced him that she was her husband's only lawful wife and she got in.

On the morning of May 1, 1905, Mr. Levy began his summing up. Except for a recess of about an hour for lunch he spoke continuously until 6:00 P.M. It was marathon achievement, skillful in its analysis of the evidence and subtle in its appeal to the feelings of the jury. It held the rapt attention of everyone in the court until the end.

It would serve little purpose here to discuss the speeches of the two lawyers in detail—much of it has already been quoted in this narrative—so I will content myself with a few excerpts to give some idea of the flavor and style of the oratory.

After paying some compliments to the judge, to his associates at the counsel table, our Anglo-American system of jurisprudence, the presumption of innocence, and the doctrine of reasonable doubt, Levy directed his attention to his opponent and to his own forensic limitations. Marc Antony himself could not have been more self-deprecating.

"I am simply a plain ordinary speaker and advocate," he said, "earnest in the cause in which I am enlisted, and not endowed with those splendid attributes that are the property of my brother on the other side. The thing I have to fear in this case is that, in considering whether or not the burden of proof has been sustained by the People, you will be fascinated and deluded, not by the sincerity and logic, but by the blandishments, powers and abilities of the learned district attorney, a gentleman of charming personality who, by his charm, will seduce your judgment . . . a gentleman who, in this case, more than any other I have seen him try, has permitted his zeal to win to overpower his usual fairness of mind. . . ."

After reminding the jurors of the mighty powers of the district attorney, Levy then continued.

"If I were district attorney of the county of New York, the most important prosecuting position in this great country of ours . . . I would not use the might of my position so exalted as that to resort to unfair methods to send a girl, defenseless, alone and poor, to her death, but I would make myself just as much her champion and protector as the counsel for the defendant."

It may be remarked in passing that Mr. Levy's female clients, regardless of age, affluence and condition of pulchritude, were almost invariably poor, defenseless girls.

In a criminal case the defense has one advantage over the prosecution: the burden of proof is on the State and the defendant is not required to prove anything. This Levy kept pounding away at throughout his speech.

"If the prosecution does not prove that Morgan Smith bought a pistol," he said, "it does not become the duty of the defendant to prove that Morgan Smith did not. If the prosecution does not prove that this girl had a guilty intention to take the life of Caesar Young, she is not called upon to open her mouth, to say a word. If the prosecution fails to prove a motive it is not the duty of the defendant to prove there was no motive."

This was of the utmost importance. The defense did not have to explain why Nan failed to take the stand but it was wise, nevertheless, to do so.

"Shall I make answer to the proposition that Morgan Smith bought a pistol upon the day of the third of June," Nan inquired rhetorically through her counsel, "when you have not proven that he did? Shall I make answer to your proposition that I killed Caesar Young, and that I planned that murder the night before, when I was awakened early in the morning from my sleep, called out by him to him, and especially when it is claimed that he had parted from me forever? No. The burden of sustaining the case is with them, and you gentlemen have sworn to decide upon the evidence. . . ."

Here his oratory became tinged with purple.

"Oh, but the learned prosecution says, 'I will wrap up this case in a wrapping that is foul, that is putrid. I will take this woman who is charged with the foulest crime known and I will cover her with filth. I will take this creature, twenty-two years of age, tenderly nurtured and reared, and I will drag her through the gutters, and I will cause her to send out a stench, so that she will be a horror to the nostrils of the twelve men whom I shall delude and mislead.

"'And what difference does it make if the evidence falls short and is insufficient to prove her guilty of murder? On general principles she is a bad woman, and they will consider the dirt with which I have covered her, and they will give no heed to the absence of the evidence I ought to have produced.'"

Having paid his compliments to his fair client and his opponent, the speaker next had a few words to say about Caesar Young.

"What is there against this girl? She was the mistress of Caesar Young. Who made her his mistress? Did Caesar Young seduce her or was he swerved from the path of rectitude by this girl who was then nineteen years old; a girl, perhaps, whose head had been turned, if you like, by the flattery that comes to those who get into the front line and enter the calcium light of the stage; a weakling—weak in the sense of being susceptible to the flattery of a strong man—a girl easily misled. . . .

"Caesar Young has been described to you as a strong man. I think that when he died he was about thirty-seven years old—an open face, a bright pleasant eye, a pleasing voice, pleasing manners, and, to his undoing, he always exercised upon women a singular fascination. 'He was a man extremely susceptible to the charms of women,' says the district attorney. 'It was inevitable that he should be with women—a loose liver. It never could be claimed that Caesar Young was a virgin or anything like that.'"

Levy seems to have been quite moved by the sad fate of his

young and virtuous client being led astray by "the man who lived by his wits; the gambler; the loose liver; the heavy drinker; the seducer—the seducer who found all women his legitimate prey; the libertine; the roué. Which picture will you have? You are the sworn judges of the facts in this case and you are going to determine which is the weaker vessel—the man or the woman."

The portrait of Nan as a "weak, easily impressed and susceptible girl, unused to the ways of the world" being led astray by a libertine and roué may come as a surprise to those who have followed this narrative attentively. Levy used to say, "You can never hope to convince a jury unless you have first convinced yourself," and this he often accomplished by astonishing feats of rationalization. I am certain that in this case, caught up in the surge of his own eloquence, he thoroughly believed every word he was saying.

But along with the flights of oratory the speech did not neglect the facts of the case. Levy's main purpose was not to convince the jury *how* Young was killed, but to suggest various possible ways by which he might have been killed. This was a case of circumstantial evidence, and if any hypothesis other than homicide was possible, Nan had to be acquitted. The speech continued.

"The next three matters which call for your consideration are the three theories advanced in this case. Did the deceased come to his death through the criminal agency of the defendant? Did Caesar Young come to his death by reason of having self-inflicted this wound—by suicide? Or, the third theory, was the death of this man encompassed by accident?"

Levy now—he had been talking effectively for two hours—proceeded to discuss in detail the testimony of the witnesses called by the prosecution. The description given by Officer Junior of Nan's behavior after Young's death was particularly useful to the defense, and the speaker used it with great histrionic effect.

"This is Junior's testimony, that the girl had the horror of the death of the man she loved pictured in her eye, with the awfulness of the situation that she was placed in before her, with her eyes staring, haggard, trembling, sobbing, wringing her hands, pale, hollow-eyed, crying, 'Caesar, Caesar, why did you do this?'

"Is there a possibility that within two seconds after hearing the shot she could have been so consummate an actress as to have been able to conceive a deliberate plan to deceive and pretend the horror that showed itself in her face at that moment? Realizing that the man to whom she had given her life and her virtue lay there, what was the most natural thing in the world for her to do but to have done as was done, to have said as was said and to have acted as was acted?

"Is there anything in this case that bears upon the shooting of Caesar Young other than is contained in the testimony of their witnesses? Junior, the policeman, saw nothing. Stemm, the boy, saw nothing. The druggist saw nothing. The cabman saw nothing."

Levy had been neglecting Rand for quite a while, so now he made up for the oversight. "How are you going to determine that this was a crime of deliberate, premeditated murder? Are you going to determine it upon the innuendo of the district attorney? Are you going to determine it upon his sneering, cutting, supercilious treatment of this unfortunate girl on trial?"

The speaker here drew a poignant contrast—the powerful

district attorney who could call upon "the great police department of the city of New York with its 9,000 men" to hunt up evidence and this "poor, poverty-stricken bit of a defenseless mite of humanity who hasn't a friend in the world outside of her poor old dad who sits outside here and her lawyers who are fighting her battle. This girl has been tried several times. Why this thirst, this lust for her blood?"

All the stops had now been pulled out; the tremolo and the *vox humana* were going strong. The speaker referred in this manner to Nan's request to Officer Quinn to hit her with his billy and kill her:

"The light of her life had gone out. The perfume of her soul had been dissipated, and she begged this policeman to kill her. . . . My learned and rhetorical and oratorical and brilliant friend will tell you that this was assumed. My God, you are all men of the world, you are men of experience. . . . Why, gentlemen of the jury, if you say that this was assumed you have got to pretend that you believe that this girl possesses ability such as has never been possessed by any artist that ever trod the boards; not even by the emotional Clara Morris, not even by the great Rachel, not even by Ristori, not even by Mrs. Leslie Carter."

Levy's lengthy speech was interspersed with homilies on the purity of womanhood, the lustful nature of man, and the fallibility of human testimony, but through it all he kept hammering away at the various possible ways by which Caesar Young might have met his death. Remember, he did not need to prove any of this. He merely had to suggest possibilities, to instill doubts in the minds of the jurors—and this he did splendidly.

As to the possibility that Young killed himself in a moment of drunkenness:

"No one can gauge the turning point between reason and unreason; no one can say when rationality ends and irrationality commences; no one can say when the impulse to take life comes. It is so in every condition. The finger of the Almighty is put upon a man's brain and can blight it in a second. No one can tell whether, in the condition the deceased was in on that morning, an impulse to suicide might have come to him, whether in a drunken frenzy or a maudlin fit."

On the possibility of accident:

"Suppose he had carried the pistol in his hip pocket. Suppose, seated in that crowded cab, he found it uncomfortable. Suppose the pistol pressed upon him and he wanted to change it from one pocket to another, and suppose that in changing it from one pocket to another it exploded . . ."

After talking for seven hours the speaker reached the limit of his endurance. "Now, gentlemen of the jury," he said, "it is my duty to close here. I feel that I have not the physical strength to continue any longer." What he feared most was that the jury might bring in a compromise verdict and find Nan guilty of a lesser degree of homicide, so he closed with a solemn admonition that the verdict had to be either murder in the first degree or not guilty.

"If you believe that her guilt has been established beyond a reasonable doubt, it is your duty to have the courage to say so. But if you have a doubt, if you say to yourselves, 'This evidence is so uncertain, it is so unsettled, I am not satisfied in my own mind, I will give a lower degree and perhaps by-

and-by something more may be found out about this matter,' you violate your oaths. You yourselves will be guilty of a greater crime than that charged against any person present in court. I say to you, no compromise! It is either guilty or not guilty!"

This was a good note upon which to end. The speech concluded with a simple and earnest peroration:

". . . I submit this case into your keeping, only adding an appeal to the Almighty Searcher of the hearts of all of us that He may search your hearts as to the rectitude of your purpose to determine this case upon the evidence, and I appeal to Him that He may give you the courage to sustain your convictions and the manliness to declare them."

CHAPTER TWENTY-SEVEN

The Prosecution Sums Up

THE COURT recessed after Mr. Levy concluded his speech at six o'clock in the evening. The following day Mr. Rand summed up to the jury. He spoke for three and a half hours.

There is a marked contrast between the two speeches. Rand's prose style was less florid than his opponent's, although he too, at times, indulged in some rather fancy rhetorical flights. His logic was more tightly knit, as indeed it had to be. His task was not to instill doubts but to dispel them; he had the burden of proof. He had to convince all twelve jurors beyond a reasonable doubt that the facts were as he stated them.

There is no doubt that his adversary's attacks had gotten under his skin. "I admired more than I can tell you," he said at the beginning of his speech, "the sublime audacity of this defendant's counsel coming before you in a case of this character, empty-handed save for the mud with which he has liberally besmirched the honest witnesses in this case and of which he has seen fit to compliment me with the lion's share. He accused me of almost every crime known to the calendar. He put me on trial at this bar for high crimes and misdemeanors committed by me as a public officer. He told you that I was a tiger thirsting for the blood of a butterfly."

Levy had not pulled his punches, but throughout his summation he had adhered to the outward forms of courtesy that for generations had been traditional at the bar and still exist in England. This was a slugging match but Levy's heaviest punches wore the verbal adornments of politeness. He invariably referred to his adversary as "Mr." Rand or "my learned opponent" or "the learned district attorney."

The battering that Rand had received the day before still hurt and he made no effort to hide his feelings. His habitual supercilious manner was heightened throughout his speech. His opponent was usually referred to contemptuously as Levy —never Mr. Levy. The sneer in his voice is audible even in the typewritten minutes of the trial. On the few occasions when he spoke of his adversary as "my learned opponent" a note of irony can be detected. It was effective retaliation but I suspect that it did not go too well with the jurors.

"Hold me to the most rigid accuracy in every word of testimony that I quote," he said bitterly. "But how about Levy? I tell you that Levy did not make a point that did not have a lie for its foundation, not one."

Rand's speech was a masterly performance of logical presentation but, paradoxically, this was, I believe, one of its weaknesses. For he staked his entire case upon the contention that Nan was guilty of murder in the first degree, a conviction for which would have meant a mandatory death sentence. He was committed to a relentless theory from which he dared not deviate.

"The Grand Jury says that Nan Patterson killed Caesar Young. Her counsel say that she did not. The facts show that if she did not he must have. So there is the simple alternative: is this murder or is it suicide? Did Caesar kill himself or did Nan Patterson kill Caesar Young? These are the propositions which must be true." Mr. Rand omitted a third possibility suggested by his adversary, that Young's death might have been caused by accident. But it would never have done for the prosecution to admit that possibility, for had he done so he would have had no case.

Rand subjected the testimony to minute analysis, piling argument upon argument forcibly and with the merciless irony with which he was at his brilliant best. On the subject of suicide:

"Now suppose you adopt Levy's suggestion that a sudden impulse came to this strong, young, rich man to kill himself, that while he rode in that cab he suddenly said to himself, 'Wouldn't it be fun to die?' and having a revolver he took it out to see how much fun it would be. And where would he naturally, being a right-handed man, shoot himself? Well, here is the brain, that is the quickest death, the roof of his mouth, the temple, the heart . . . You don't think, do you, that he would have held the revolver upside down and pulled the trigger with his thumb? You don't suppose that having suddenly decided to die and knowing how fatal a shot in the heart would be, you don't suppose that he was going to shoot himself through the apex of his left lung to the fourth dorsal vertebra?"

The persuasiveness of this is irresistible. Rand had shot the defense suggestion of suicide full of holes. Didn't it then follow inexorably that if Young hadn't killed himself Nan must have killed him?

Rand was puzzled, as Levy had been, by the postcard that Young had given to Nan. It was his contention that Young had written it, not in the saloon, but in the cab. This was evidenced by the shaky handwriting. He then advanced the astonishing suggestion that Nan had deliberately murdered her companion while he was in the act of writing the card.

"This is a souvenir postal card he had in his pocket. I haven't the faintest idea but that he was going to send it back by the pilot, and I haven't any doubt that this was the moment that she chose to kill him—while he was writing that postal card."

There was no evidence of this. Rand was, in effect, accusing Nan of having murdered her companion in cold blood, and whatever force there was in his suggestion it could only have had the effect of making it more difficult for the jury to bring in a verdict of guilty.

I have already said that the greatest weakness in the prosecution's case was the absence of proof of motive. The conspiracy in which the Smiths were supposed to have participated was left vague throughout the trial. This is what Rand said about it:

"Now, gentlemen, I never said, in opening this case, that I could prove there was a conspiracy to extort money from Caesar Young. Never have I said in any place any such thing. I said I would prove there was a conspiracy to separate him from his wife and keep him with this defendant. Whether that was for the sake of the money there was in it I leave you to say."

Just how this was to be accomplished with a loaded revolver he did not explain. Young had written many letters to Nan when she was in California, and the prosecutor now argued that Nan was keeping them as a possible means of blackmail if Young should discard her. Nan had previously denied on the witness stand that she had any letters—but Rand contended that the reason Young wanted to see her on the night of June third and again on the morning of June fourth was to make a last effort to get them back from her. It seems hardly likely that he expected Nan to have the letters with her in the hansom cab. Rand next took up the conversation in Flannery's saloon:

"Luce is dismissed from the stand without a word of cross-examination, an admission that he is an honest and truthful man and has told you only the truth."

Of course it was an admission of nothing of the sort, as the assistant district attorney well knew. But the Marquis of Queensberry rules did not prevail in this contest and there was plenty of hitting below the belt on both sides. At any rate, Levy did not object and the point, no doubt, registered with the jury.

When he came to Nan's supposed threat in the saloon, Rand's prose style became more lyrical:

"Oh, gentlemen, this case is growing now in sadness. Oh, the shadows gather here. When you come to take up the question of premeditation, what are you going to say about that statement of hers to Caesar Young, 'You will never sail tomorrow morning for I will be there to stop you'?"

He then spoke of the scene outside the saloon when Young slapped her and said he would knock her goddamned head off:

"He was getting mad at this time and slapped her, struck her. Do you think that blow cooled her purpose? Do you think that blow abated her design? Ah, a few hours before, Morgan Smith had told her that she had got to do it and she still hesitated for she said, 'I won't.' But when she drove home to her hotel that night the blow of Caesar Young and his curse had done what the blow and curse of Morgan Smith could not do. Do you doubt that when Young went to his sleep that night he was a man marked for slaughter?"

Rand had now gone all out. He was asking the jury unequivocally to send Nan to the electric chair, and he was asking them to believe that she had determined, the night before, to murder Young because he had slapped and cursed her. This was a lot to ask any jury to swallow.

The prosecutor now turned to Morgan Smith and the testimony of the newsboy, Hewitt. I have already quoted Rand's statement regarding Smith:

"Here he has been day after day in court. Oh, gentlemen, it is so sickening, it is such rubbish to ask you to suppose that these people were not privy to the design to shoot Caesar Young."

If this does not mean that Rand was accusing Smith and his wife of conspiring with Nan to take Young's life, I don't know what it means.

Turning to the purchase of the revolver, the prosecutor launched into a superb satirical passage. This was the vein in which he was at his best.

"I did say in my opening that the revolver was bought at the pawnshop of Hyman Stern on the third day of June 1904 by J. Morgan Smith, and over that proposition my learned friend [one of the few times Rand so referred to his opponent] has gone into a perfect spasm of hysterical amazement and surprise. He stands amazed, he tells you, at the unparalleled audacity of my making such a statement and then not proving it to your satisfaction.

"Well, gentlemen of the jury, you must not take Levy too seriously. Levy has been standing amazed so long that he really has forgotten how to stand any other way. Every ruling of the court amazed Levy. Every jury with its verdict amazes Levy. Why, it is my firm belief that when Levy was born into the world he stood amazed and he has never outgrown that condition of amazement, at least we have never seen him in any other condition and I have seen him in many cases, in many trials.

"I suppose that when my eyes shall be turned to behold for the last time this now familiar courtroom scene, the figure that will arrest every gaze will be, not that of the venerable judge, holding with such exact and equal poise the scales of justice; not that of the jury as they stand in obedience to the call of the court to deliver their true and honest verdict; but Levy, standing at the bar of justice, amazed that any jury could convict a client of his.

"Nay, who can doubt that on that last great day, when from the throne of the Almighty the last judgment is pronounced, solitary and aloof from the approving chorus of the angels of God, his wings outspread, in helpless indignation, the cherub Levy will stand amazed."

We can be sure that the jurors and the large audience that crowded the courtroom chuckled at this brilliant *tour de force*. I am positive, too, that no one there enjoyed and appreciated it as much as Rand's adversary against whom it was directed.

Unfortunately the prosecutor's wit was sharper than his proof.

"I never said that Stern would say that Morgan Smith bought the revolver," he asserted. "I said that Morgan Smith bought it and now I will prove that to your complete satisfaction." This he utterly failed to do.

Rand candidly admitted that the pawnbroker, Hyman Stern, was an honest witness. He said: "I think he is an honest citizen; I thoroughly concede that . . . I don't believe there is any reason to suspect his integrity at all. In the first place, he is a very nearsighted man. You saw that by the difficulty he had in giving the number of the revolver. You saw the glasses he wore. This whole transaction, I suppose, occupied only a very few minutes—the sale of a ten-dollar revolver. There was nothing at the time in the circumstances of the purchase particularly to attract his attention."

Pawnbrokers, Rand said, do not sell loaded revolvers, so after the gun was purchased bullets had to be obtained. It was his belief, he told the jury, that when Morgan Smith and Nan went over to Healy's to get Young's telephone message, they stopped at some shop in the neighborhood and bought the bullets.

The evidence that would prove conclusively that Morgan Smith had bought the revolver was not, he asserted, in the testimony of Stern but in the testimony of Smith's wife, Julia. Rand had asked her where she was on June eighth and she had refused to answer.

"What is the significance in this case of the eighth day of June? I wonder if you have forgotten. I wonder if you have forgotten that it was on the eighth day of June that Stern, the pawnbroker who sold the gun, was discovered and was brought down to the district attorney's office. That is why I wanted to know where Julia Smith and her husband were on the eighth day of June."

That was the day before the Smiths ran away. Rand could not say so, for the fact was not in evidence, but the jury knew perfectly well what he was driving at. He then referred to the letter that Julia had written to Nan the night before she was arrested in Cincinnati. This was the letter that had been excluded from evidence, in which there was mention of someone referred to as "S." Julia had refused to tell who "S" was on the ground that an answer might convict her of a crime. Rand continued:

"What crime? What crime, I wonder, could Julia Smith be concerned in that would be shown by her admitting that she used the word *Stern* in a letter. Is there any suggestion of any crime she might be concerned in except the purchase of this revolver? Talk about circumstantial evidence! Why, if fifty Sterns had testified they saw Morgan Smith buy the gun it could not be half as persuasive as Julia Smith's attitude with regard to that question upon this trial."

Rand's logic was sound but unfortunately he was obliged to draw inferences from matter that had been left out of the record. Julia's attitude was not evidence. There was no proof that the Smiths had run away on June eighth. And Julia's letter to Nan was not in the record.

One of the odd features of the case was that on the morning of his expected departure Young had called up Nan and had come down from 140th Street to meet her at Columbus Circle. Here is Rand's explanation:

"He may not have wished to have the final parting with her

take the shape of a curse and a blow. He was a warmhearted man, a man of generous sympathies, they tell you, not a man who would have that kind of final parting with the woman he had once loved. But, more important to my mind, and the best reason, and what I really believe was the true reason, was that this woman had threatened to stop his going at the boat, and he wanted to prevent a scene at the boat. . . . Do you remember—I ask you to remember it here—what his orders were on each occasion to the cabman? Never 'Drive to the White Star pier.' Never 'Drive to the foot of West Fulton Street.' 'Drive me down to Fulton Street.' . . . Someone had to see Nan Patterson that morning or she would have been at the boat and there would have been a scene there. Now take your choice of these reasons. How can we tell which was the real one? Any one of them is reason enough."

As Rand approached the close of his speech, his oratory became more fervid:

"Oh gentlemen, gentlemen, we are near the end—we are near the end now. Never, never in his life had Caesar Young been so strong and rich as on that morning of the fourth day of June—so strong that he could push away a mountain; so rich that he could deck the marble stone with pearls; strong in the strength of a man from whose soul has been lifted the brand of shame; rich in the hope of that strength; rich in the love of the noble wife, and happy in his anticipation of celebrating his reunion by a holiday with her. Going back to revisit his old home and his old friends, a richer, stronger, happier man than Caesar Young that morning you shall not find. But it was not so ordered in the book of fate. The harvest of the seed he had sown had still to be reaped, and the name of the reaper was Nan Patterson.

"And his companion—what were her thoughts, what were her reflections as she sat there by his side? Can you open her soul? I cannot but we know what she was, we know what she had been, we know the condition that the thought of separation from Young put her in, for her own words have told us. As well might one attempt to arrest and hold the shapes that crowd the dreams that maddening narcotics have driven through the brain of man as try to picture the furies that dance and rave in the sick fancy of a jealous woman.

"But one call, you may be sure, was insistent in her thoughts, one call heard again and again. 'You have lost, Nan. You have lost. The end has come; your rival has triumphed; the wife has won; the mistress has lost; and you have lost your handsome, generous lover. No more riots, no more love with him. He is going back, he is going back. Caesar is going back, Nan, back, back to his true love. Caesar is going back, Nan, back, back to the woman who had shared his poverty, who had saved his money, who has adorned his wealth. Back, Caesar is going back to the wife he had sworn before God to love, honor and cherish.'

"Oh, if she had doubts they vanished then. Then she saw red. Then the murder in her heart flamed into action and she shot and killed. A little crack, a little puff of smoke, a dead man prostrate on a woman's knee. The wages of sin were paid."

Here Rand showed that he too was addicted to the lush oratory of the period. The passage probably sounded less banal than it reads, and the jury undoubtedly loved it.

At the end of his speech he hedged slightly from his insistence upon a first-degree verdict.

"Her counsel has told you . . . that you have but a single

alternative. He concedes to you that if this defendant killed Caesar Young she meant to do it, she planned to do it, and she is guilty of murder in the first degree. Gentlemen, with that opinion of learned counsel I agree. But you, gentlemen of the jury, are not bound by our agreement. It is not for us to say of what crime is this defendant guilty. It is for you."

Rand had to be consistent in his demand for a first-degree verdict, but he realized that there was little likelihood that all twelve jurors would agree to send Nan to her death in the electric chair. However, there was a strong possibility that the jury might bring in a compromise verdict—a verdict of homicide in one of the lower degrees. This would have meant a prison sentence for Nan, which would have been a great victory for Rand. It was what his opponent feared most. At the Hotel Metropole that afternoon several bets were made that Nan would be found guilty of manslaughter.

CHAPTER TWENTY-EIGHT

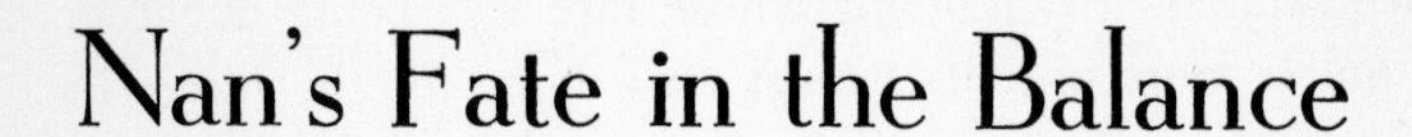

Nan's Fate in the Balance

AFTER MR. RAND finished his summing up, Recorder Goff delivered his charge and the jury retired to deliberate on Nan's fate. For several blocks in the vicinity of the courthouse the streets were black with people who had been gathered there all day and who waited anxiously for a verdict during the thirteen hours of deliberation.

At about seven o'clock the jurors were sent out by the judge to a nearby restaurant for dinner. To pass through the milling crowd was something of a problem. The New York *Times* said:

> The jurymen while on their way to and from a restaurant in Park Row were jogged and jostled by the crowd that packed the streets. All the way to the restaurant the jurymen heard yells of "Free Nan Patterson!" "Nan's all right!" "She's done nothing wrong!" "You let her loose!"

Years ago a play, *The Witching Hour*, posed the question of the psychic effect upon the deliberation of a jury of thousands of people around the country praying and hoping for the acquittal of a defendant whose fate was being debated. How much more potent it must have been for the jurors in the Nan Patterson case actually to hear the shouts and pleas of the mob crowding about them.

The jury returned from dinner and resumed their deliberations. At 1:40 A.M. the foreman sent word to the judge that they were unable to agree. Recorder Goff sent for the jury and after briefly reminding them of the importance of the case urged them to make another effort to come to an agreement.

At 2:30 in the morning the jury sent another communication to the judge. Mr. Levy had gone home and the defense was represented by his associate, Mr. O'Reilly. When Recorder Goff ascended the bench, the defendant was not in court.

"Where is she?" he asked.

"She is ill," a court officer replied. "I went over to the Tombs myself and I was told that she was quite ill."

"Well, go over again and bring her here if she is able to come," Goff said. A short while later a deputy sheriff came into the court and reported that Nan was being dressed by the matron. After a delay of about ten minutes, which seemed much longer to the reporters and spectators waiting tensely in the courtroom, Nan was brought over from the Tombs to the courtroom.

She staggered toward her accustomed chair, but she was assisted over to the railing, where she stood ashen and trembling.

"She was on the verge of collapse," said the New York *Times,* "and could hardly drag one foot after the other. An attendant on each side fairly lifted her into her place."

The judge then read the message he had received from the jury:

" 'After careful consideration of all the evidence in the case we have reached a point where we believe there is no likelihood that we shall agree.'

"Is there any possibility that you could reach a verdict after further deliberation?" the Recorder asked.

"So far as I am concerned my mind is clear. I cannot speak for the others," the foreman answered.

Goff was plainly displeased and he put the same question to each juror separately. Each answered in turn, "There is no hope of an agreement."

"Have you anything to say, Mr. Rand?"

"Nothing."

"Or you, Mr. O'Reilly?"

"Nothing."

Then, curtly, without a word of comment, Recorder Goff told the jury that they were discharged. The trial of Nan Patterson was ended. Ended, but she was not yet free. The jury had not acquitted her.

As the jurors filed out of the jury box, Nan fell from her chair in a faint. Mr. O'Reilly and the guards and attendants carried her out of the courtroom.

The aftermath was reported the next day in the New York *World:*

> After the Recorder had discharged the jury yesterday morning court officers picked up Nan Patterson in her chair and carried her to the prison pen. She was unconscious, moaning,

> calling for her father and mother. Her face was ashen pale. They carried her down to the Bridge of Sighs and across it. During her absence from her cell Mrs. Smith had been anxiously waiting for some word from the jury room. She heard the tramping of feet and the voices of the men who were bearing her sister across the prison yard. Soon they carried what appeared to her like her sister's dead body into the cell.
>
> "Nan! My sister Nan!" she cried. "Oh, what has happened? Oh, why don't you speak to me?"
>
> Daniel O'Reilly just then rushed in and explained that in all probability she did not know that the jury had disagreed and had been discharged.
>
> The women undressed the unconscious girl, put her to bed, and applied restoratives, but in vain.
>
> "The best thing to do," said Mr. O'Reilly, "is to leave her as she is and let her sleep. That is all she needs."
>
> Deputy Warden Hanley and Warden Flynn on their rounds at seven o'clock looked into the hospital cell where the two sisters are.
>
> "What a picture!" said the warden. Nan Patterson lay sound asleep, breathing heavily. Kneeling at her side was Julia Smith, sound asleep with her arm under her sister's waist.

The following morning Mr. Levy and Mr. O'Reilly visited Nan. "Well, Nan, little girl," Mr. Levy said cheerfully, "how are you this morning?"

"Oh, tell me, Mr. Levy," she said, "what has happened? It must be something awful!" She did not realize what had occurred. Her lawyers explained to her that the jury had failed to agree and that she would soon be free, but she refused to believe them. Later in the day when one of the clerks from Levy and Unger visited her, she again asked what had happened. She still was unable to understand that there had not been a verdict of guilty.

All that day letters and telegrams poured into the Tombs. Many were messages of congratulation; some were offers of bail in any amount; there were also a number containing offers from theatrical managers; and during that day and for several days following Nan received dozens of offers of marriage.

As the jurors left the courthouse after the disagreement, they were surrounded by reporters but they refused to speak. They said that they had agreed not to reveal anything that had taken place in the jury room, but after a day or so they changed their minds.

It might be mentioned in passing that, contrary to popular opinion, there is no prohibition, even though admonished by the judge not to do so, against jurors talking about what occurred in the jury room, once the case is over.

An article that appeared in the New York *World* of May 11, 1904, will be of interest, not only to the general reader, but especially to trial lawyers who are concerned with that baffling psychological mystery: What makes jurors behave the way they do?

> The Nan Patterson jury at the time of discharge stood eight in favor of acquittal and four for conviction of the crime of manslaughter in the first degree.
>
> They reached this decision on the third formal ballot and remained deadlocked thereafter. From the beginning the jury was unanimous in the belief that the woman did not intentionally shoot Young.
>
> A majority believed that Young did not commit suicide, that the girl and not Young was in possession of the gun when they entered the cab, and that it was discharged accidentally during a struggle.
>
> A majority of the jurors reached the conclusion that the

girl had pretended or threatened to attempt her own life and that Young met his death while trying to save her.

The minority held that she had tried to frighten him by pointing the revolver at him without intent to shoot, and that as he attempted to wrest the weapon from her it was accidentally discharged. This, they held, would constitute manslaughter in the first degree. At least two jurors thought it possible that Young had committed suicide.

On the first ballot the jury stood six for acquittal and six against acquittal. When the result was announced one of the jurymen, with a sigh of relief, exclaimed, "Well, thank God there is no chance of sending that girl to the electric chair."

"I'm glad to find that I'm not alone in my opinion," exclaimed another juror who had voted for acquittal. "My conviction is so strong that I would have to stand my ground if I voted alone."

A third juror interposed rather testily: "I don't believe any one of us believes there was murder in the first degree, but I'm satisfied that the revolver did not belong to Young and I think that there was manslaughter to say the least."

"It seems to me you are reasoning backward," interposed one of the strongest advocates for acquittal, speaking for the first time. "You, in substance, admit the shooting was unintentional, and if that is true there is nothing in the evidence to show who was at fault. For all we know this girl may have been simply showing Young the revolver."

After lunch a second ballot was taken in which Juror Number Eleven joined those for acquittal, increasing their strength to seven. At the suggestion of the foreman the question of the ownership of the revolver was taken up.

"While the actual purchaser of the revolver has not been identified," one of the jurors argued, "it has been shown that it was purchased on June third, the day before the killing, at a time when Young himself could not possibly have bought it. In this connection we have the right, according to the Recorder, to take into consideration the action of the Morg

Smiths and the refusal of Mrs. Smith to answer questions on the ground that her answers might incriminate her."

Others held that even if it were clearly established that Nan Patterson took the pistol with her on the morning of the shooting there was nothing to show that she intended to murder or that she had the pistol when it was discharged.

When the possibility that Young had committed suicide was under discussion one of the jurors, at the request of the others, put on the coat and waistcoat worn by Young when he was shot. He demonstrated to his own satisfaction that he could shoot holes in the coat. "Gentlemen," said this juror, "there is nothing in Mr. Rand's statement that suicide is out of the question. That is the end of this business for me. There is the basis of a reasonable doubt."

They took the third formal ballot soon after dinner at 9:55 P.M. and it was found that Juror Number Two had come over for acquittal.

In vain did the eight argue with the four who stood out for conviction. They held that the girl had a motive for shooting, and, whether she intended to kill Young or not, she was certainly responsible for his death.

"She ought to be punished," said the spokesman for the four, "and we are for manslaughter."

"You talk like a fool," said one of the jurors hotly, and that was the nearest to a quarrel that the jury came.

After the jury had been called out and sent back by the Recorder the foreman asked the four minority jurors if there was any chance of their coming to an agreement by further argument. They replied that their minds were made up. The matter was settled by a speech from one of the jurymen who had been for acquittal from the first.

"I can never vote for conviction," he said. "The case against the girl has not been proved and there is a clear basis for reasonable doubt. Rand's argument was largely made up of bluster and we might as well tell the Recorder we are wasting the time of the court and the county. I want to sleep comfortably the rest of my life and I never could do it if I sent this girl to prison."

"That settles it," was the decision of all.

It is rare that outsiders are privileged to listen in on the secret deliberations of a jury and this report presents a fascinating clinical study of the Anglo-American jury system in action. How much the jurors were swayed by Mr. Levy's fervid periods or Mr. Rand's savage invective is impossible to determine. Probably more than they were conscious of.

But we can see that when the jurors settled down to perform their sworn task, they stripped the case of its nonessentials and applied themselves to an intelligent and conscientious analysis of the evidence. To those of us who believe devoutly in trial by jury it is heartening to read this account.

Ten days had passed since the jury disagreed but Nan was still in a hospital cell in the Tombs. There was loud clamor in the press for her immediate release, but Mr. Jerome, who was not to be rushed, stated that he was checking the vote of the jury and that if the vote had been preponderantly in favor of acquittal he would consent to her discharge.

On the morning of Friday, May 12, Nan made her last journey across the Bridge of Sighs. She was not taken into the courtroom but waited in the adjacent pen. Before Recorder Goff were District Attorney Jerome, his assistants Rand and Garvan, Abraham Levy, Henry W. Unger, and Daniel O'Reilly. Jerome arose and addressed the court. There was evident sternness and chagrin in his remarks.

"This case has been misrepresented to the public," he said, "and the trial has resulted in a miscarriage of justice. I have looked at the trial in all its aspects. I have no criticism to make of the judge or the jury. They performed their duty."

However, Mr. Jerome went on, the press had been unfair. The trials had not cost between $200,000 and $300,000 as the newspapers had stated but only $8,000, and he had an auditor's report to prove it.

He then launched into a defense of Rand. "Whatever he did in my opinion he did right—he did bravely, efficiently and well. I ask that the defendant be discharged on her own recognizance. Another trial would be unavailing."

"The motion is granted," said Recorder Goff.

CHAPTER TWENTY-NINE

"Are There Any More at Home Like You?"

THE JOYOUS TIDINGS were heralded to the world by an exultant press. In headlines that covered half of the front page the *Evening Journal* announced:

NAN FREE
DISCHARGED BY GOFF
WITHOUT BAIL

In red letters at the foot of the page was this further commentary:

2,000 CHEER NAN AS
SHE QUITS TOMBS

Nan Patterson was greeted by a crowd of 2,000 cheering people when she left the Criminal Courts Building after her release today.

She was led through the corridors of the building, the po-

> lice vainly trying to keep back the weeping women and shouting men who struggled to clasp the girl's hands.
>
> A tremendous shout went up when the girl, between her old father and Lawyer Levy, appeared in the street at the Franklin Street entrance to the Criminal Courts Building.
>
> A carriage was waiting and a great crowd pursued the carriage as it went back of the Tombs down Elm Street to Mr. Levy's office in Park Row where final preparations for Nan's departure for Washington were made.

The news of Nan's liberation caused a widespread rejoicing that is hard to explain. Why the discharge of a chorus girl who had been accused of murdering her lover should have been welcomed with as much joy as if the Messiah had unexpectedly walked out of the Tombs is a question of mass insanity that I will leave to psychologists. I well remember, and so will many people my age, the children in the street singing happily to the tune of "Tammany":

Nan is free, Nan is free.
She escaped the electric chair,
Now she's out in the open air . . .

Some of the kids sang a less friendly but equally jubilant version. The second line of the song was gleefully rendered, "She deserved the electric chair."

Nan remained in Washington for a week with her ailing mother, who for the past ten months had been on the verge of dying whenever the newspapers were short of news, but who had nevertheless managed miraculously to survive the three trials.

On May 18 the New York *American* reported that Nan had returned to New York to go on the stage. Hurtig and Seamon, well-known theatrical producers, had signed her up to appear in one of their vaudeville theaters. The same edition of the newspaper had also this interesting item:

> Mrs. Caesar Young sailed for Europe yesterday accompanied by John B. Millin, her late husband's racing partner. She was registered as Mrs. Jacob Becker and he as John Becker. They will be married in London is the report.

So Mrs. Young got her trip abroad at last, and the devoted Millin got his reward. Imperial Caesar, dead and turned to clay . . .

The harrowing experience that Nan had gone through and her tender reunion with her aged mother had mellowed and matured her. After she left her lawyer's office and returned to the St. Paul Hotel, she went out with her rejoicing friends to celebrate. When she returned to New York, she was still celebrating. This is the report in the *American* of her return from Washington:

> Nan Patterson returned to New York last night to begin "the new life" for which she had prayed so eloquently while in her cell in the Tombs prison. She began her chastened existence by visiting Broadway restaurants in an automobile with a merry party.

Well, one can hardly begrudge a girl a night or two of innocent relaxation after spending long, weary months behind the bars. The *American* continued its account:

> Nan arrived in Jersey City on the Congressional Limited over the Pennsylvania Railroad at 8:55 o'clock. Nan's chaperone was her sister, Mrs. Harriet C. Lowell. When she and her sister stepped from the train they crossed the tracks to an elevator which took them to the street where an auto, provided, it was said, by Hurtig and Seamon, was waiting.
>
> It is with Hurtig and Seamon and other business agents

> that Nan Patterson has signed contracts containing most unusual stipulations. They are in the nature of pledges of her good behavior for a year.
>
> She has agreed over her own signature not to drink any intoxicating liquors for one year; not to visit any saloons or cafés where liquor is sold during the period; and never to appear upon the public streets without a chaperone.
>
> Mrs. Patterson, mother of Nan, was selected as the best person to take charge of her, but Mrs. Patterson refused to accept the position.
>
> The unusual restrictions were placed in the contracts with the former *Floradora* girl because of the experience Harry Seamon had on the night Nan Patterson was liberated from the Tombs. Mr. Seamon is willing to help Nan Patterson but he does not want to present her as an attraction at the Hurtig and Seamon theaters unless she is subjected to control. Nan Patterson is, according to the terms of the contract, to receive $2,000 from Hurtig & Seamon for the first week, and the recompense thereafter is to depend upon the success of her first week's performance.

We are not informed what experience Mr. Seamon had on the night of Nan's liberation but we are permitted to speculate.

Nan made her debut in vaudeville at Hurtig and Seamon's theater, and I was there. I remember her vividly, pompadoured and buxom, clad in an attractive pink dress—a striking contrast to the deep mourning costume in which I had last seen her in the courtroom. She stood in the spotlight before the curtain and sang a song called "That's What the Daisy Said."

One I love, two I love,
Three I love I say.
Four I love with all my heart,
And five I cast away—

As she sang she plucked the petals from a daisy and tossed them to the audience. She was terrible.

She told the newspapers that she had gone on the stage to pay her lawyer's fee and this Mr. Levy deeply resented; he stated that he would not accept money for his services which might be raised by Nan Patterson in this way. "I am not a party to any theatrical contracts," he said. "I disapprove of all that Nan Patterson has done since she left the Tombs. I am through with this case forever. I went into this case through a misunderstanding as to the payment of my fee, but I felt in duty bound to remain as counsel for the girl. I want no girl to work to pay me my fee, and what I have done for this girl stands on record as having been done without compensation."*

Nan Patterson's career in vaudeville was, as I have indicated, somewhat less than sensational. To the indefatigable Alexander Woollcott I am indebted for the following footnote to her career: "It was immediately announced that Nan would be starred in a musical show called *The Lulu Girls.* It opened shortly thereafter in Scranton, Pennsylvania, and got as far as Altoona when, although billed by that time as *A Romance of Panama,* it quietly expired. Shortly thereafter Nan was remarried, after a lively vacation, to an early husband from whom she had been obscurely divorced."

The "early husband" was young Leon Gaines Martin, who

* If I may again add my own testimony, Father told me many times that he never received a cent for defending Nan Patterson. I would like to add, too, that after Nan walked out of his office on the day of her discharge from the Tombs he never saw her or heard from her again.

had been a faithful visitor during Nan's residence in the Tombs. They were remarried on September 16, 1905.

Nan's name continued to appear in the newspapers but with diminishing frequency. She was still good copy but new idols were being raised for the adoration of the populace. On the night of June 26, 1906, a little more than a year after Nan's liberation, a Pittsburgh multimillionaire named Harry K. Thaw shot and killed, in the roof garden on top of Madison Square Garden, the world-famous architect Stanford White. The motive, it was said, was that White had seduced Thaw's wife, a beautiful young model named Evelyn Nesbit.

A new and glamorous heroine had appeared on the scene, and the case of Nan Patterson softly faded into legend.

CHAPTER THIRTY

. . . And Afterward

WITHOUT ENDEAVORING to separate fact from fiction, it will be of interest to recount here some of the stories told of Nan's subsequent history.

In August 1905 the sister-in-law of a wealthy Duluth broker, C. Ralph Ash, declared indignantly that Nan was making an energetic play for the susceptible Mr. Ash and his bankroll. According to the report, his relatives stepped in and blighted this incipient romance.

Then, in 1906, there appeared a story that Nan had won the heart of a wealthy iron magnate, residing in the outskirts of Pittsburgh. At the instigation of his jealous wife the police intervened and ordered Nan's deportation from town. Nan appealed to the mayor, who called off the constabulary and saved her from banishment.

About a year later a prominent resident of Pittsburgh, Dr. John Brittyn, killed himself. The newspapers insisted that he had committed suicide because Nan had rejected his suit. By this time she was beginning to be fed up, so she sent an indignant communication to the newspapers: "I have been mixed up in stories with all sorts of people," she said. "All of them were lies. First it was an iron man; now it is a doctor; and next, I suppose, they will have me connected with a chauffeur or a masseur. I don't know anything about Brittyn's suicide, and I care less about it. Please let me alone for a time."

Nan, for a while, had her wish and was permitted to live in obscurity. Sometime during this interval she must have again divorced Martin, for the next we hear of her is that on December 10, 1910, in Marinette, Wisconsin, the local newspaper announced the marriage of Ann E. Martin to Captain Summer K. Prescott. Ann E. Martin was Nan Patterson. Her new husband had served with distinction in the Spanish–American War. He was the son of a rich manufacturer and was an officer in his father's company.

Sometime in the nineteen-twenties a story appeared in the newspapers that a washwoman in Yonkers had gotten into a violent row with a neighbor. The Yonkers newspapers stated that the belligerent lady was Nan Patterson, and the story appeared in many newspapers and magazines all over the country.

"One of these papers," said the New York *Sunday News* in a magazine article published in 1923, "was dropped on the stoop of a handsome home at No. 4009 Point Street, Seattle, Washington.

"In that house, overlooking Puget Sound, was a woman who had been living happily for ten years with the friendship and good will of her neighbors as the wife of a rich and able manufacturer. The woman who picked up the lurid story of the washtub row was none other than Nan Patterson herself, astonished to find her alter ego performing before a washboard 3,000 miles away."

And that is the last we hear of Nan Patterson. If she is alive today, and she may well be, she would be a woman of seventy-six. It is pleasing to picture her in the sunset of her life, silver-haired and tranquil, alone with her memories as she looks across the waters of Puget Sound. I wonder if there runs through her mind the refrain of an old, familiar song, "For I must love someone, really, and it might as well be you."

CHAPTER THIRTY-ONE

How It Might Have Happened

FIFTY-FOUR YEARS have passed since Caesar Young died and the riddle of what happened in the hansom cab on that fatal morning of June 4, 1904, is still unsolved. How did Caesar Young die? And, what is even more puzzling, why did he die?

I believe that we can rule out at once the hypothesis that Nan Patterson murdered him. For if this was murder it was, as Mr. Rand contended, premeditated and deliberate, and the supposition that Nan was a deliberate killer is psychologically fantastic. Nan may or may not have been in love with Young, but as I see her she was not a girl capable of an intense, romantic passion. She doubtless cared for him after her fashion but she was not a tragic heroine who would kill because of blighted affection.

Moreover, she had no conceivable motive for killing Young, and this was one of the great weaknesses of the prosecution's case. Young was her meal ticket. He represented to her a life of gaiety, ease and self-indulgence, and there still remained the possibility that she might win him back. She had every reason to want him to remain alive. As Al Smith once said: "One does not shoot Santa Claus."

Rand's suggestion that she murdered in a spirit of resentment is even more absurd than that she killed because of a broken heart. It is preposterous to believe that when Young slapped her in the face in the early hours of June fourth he was then, as Rand contended, "a man marked for slaughter."

I am convinced that Nan was not a murderer. I am equally certain that Caesar Young was not a suicide. Even if it were true, as Levy suggested, that he was morose and despondent because of financial losses and the prospect of a temporary separation from his mistress, and was maudlin because of excessive drinking, it is psychologically incredible that he would take his own life. He was young, vigorous, pleasure-loving and incapable of any profound depth of feeling. This was no Romeo and Juliet affair.

All the evidence negatives the likelihood of suicide: his insistence upon putting a warm suit in the trunk to wear on the steamer; his direction to the cab driver to be at the pier at nine o'clock; and the purchase of a new hat just before he was shot. A man does not buy a new hat in which to kill himself.

The nature of the wound and the course of the bullet also strongly contradict the likelihood of suicide. Of course he could have shot himself, as Levy ingeniously demonstrated, by reaching his right hand over to his left shoulder and pulling the trigger with his thumb, but a man does not go through such awkward acrobatics when he can conveniently blow his brains out or shoot himself in the heart.

To me the most persuasive evidence that Young did not take his own life is the fact that Nan unquestionably lied on the witness stand. There was, of course, much perjury on both sides, but the false testimony of the only living eyewitness was the most significant. Nan *knew* what took place in the cab. She said that Young shot himself, which was palpably untrue, so she must have had a strong reason for concealing the actual facts.

Caesar and Nan were seated side by side in a compartment not much larger than a telephone booth. However the pistol was discharged, one thing is certain: it went off a few inches from her ear. It must have exploded with a sound almost loud enough to shatter her eardrums. Stemm, standing on the sidewalk some distance away, recognized the sound as a pistol shot and immediately saw smoke coming out of the cab. Michaels, sitting outside above the roof, said that he heard a loud report.

But Nan, with the pistol exploding almost in her ear, swore that she heard "a muffled sound—smothered. At first I thought it came from the street. Then I saw the smoke." Even more incredible is her statement on direct examination: "I then heard a muffled sound. I saw no pistol. He half raised himself again and I began to scold him, not realizing what had happened." How could anyone in his right mind be expected to believe that? This is so clearly false that one wonders that the jury at the second trial did not reject her testimony in its entirety and promptly find her guilty.

Her story of immediately looking for the gun and finding it in Young's right-hand coat pocket is one that must have strained the credulity of the jurors. Is it conceivable that a woman, stunned by the shock of an unexpected tragedy, would have had the self-possession to search for the weapon in the pocket of her prostrate companion? What earthly difference did it make to her at that moment where the gun was?

And that brings us to the supreme riddle in the case. Why was there a loaded revolver in the cab that morning and how did it get there? We can never know the correct answers; we can only guess. And my guess is that the key to the mystery can be found in the bizarre personality of Nan's brother-in-law, J. Morgan Smith.

Smith was never a witness and he never made any statements to the reporters, but we know enough about him to be able to draw a fairly plausible picture of him.

He was a big, florid man in his thirties, addicted to liquor and gambling. Ostensibly he was an insurance broker, but there is little indication that he ever devoted any time to the insurance business. He appears to have had many of Caesar Young's amiable vices, but he lacked Young's talent to earn money to gratify them.

We know that during the period with which we are concerned Smith was usually hard up and that at times he had to resort to pawning his wife's jewelry for small amounts. When he was arrested in Cincinnati he was so broke that the meals of himself and his wife had to be provided through the generosity of the district attorney.

All this lends color to Rand's contention—which he never could prove—that the Smiths had been living for some time off the bounty of Caesar Young. There was a strong bond of affection between the Patterson sisters. Young had been lavishly generous to Nan, and we can be pretty sure that the Smiths were taken care of out of the money he gave her.

This happy state of affairs Morgan Smith believed was going to continue. Young had told Julia many times that he was going to divorce his wife and marry Nan. The Smiths would have a rich and indulgent brother-in-law, and for Morgan life would continue to be a gay round of boozing and gambling and Caesar would pay the bills.

Suddenly this delightful prospect was threatened. Coggins' visit to Julia was a danger warning that could not be ignored. Nan must have sensed that her hold upon Young was loosening, although she still had confidence in the seductive power of her physical attractions; but when Julia said that Nan, upon her arrival in New York, was on the verge of hysteria, she was undoubtedly telling the truth.

Something had to be done and done quickly, for the omens presaged bad news not only for Nan but for the pleasure-loving Smiths. Julia, who was by all odds the cleverest actor in this drama, promptly sat down and wrote a letter to Young that was both appealing and subtly threatening. If Caesar did not do right by her sister, Nan might do something serious either to herself or to him.

It is possible that Nan knew about the sending of this letter, but Rand was unable to prove it and that is why Judge Goff excluded it from the case. What she and Julia could not have anticipated was that Mrs. Young would intercept it. Mrs. Young, in court, passed over the episode lightly, but we can rest assured that a violent scene ensued when Caesar arrived at the Hotel Walcott that evening. Here was proof positive that Nan and her sister were still striving desperately to steal her husband from her. Poor Caesar was indeed on the spot. He saw Nan that night and apparently placated her, but if she had not known it before she must have known from that moment on that her grip on Young was slipping. What is equally important, Julia and Morgan knew it too.

Mrs. Young and Millin were putting pressure on Young on one side, Nan was exerting her siren charms on the other, and Caesar was uncomfortably trapped in the middle. He tried to extricate himself by trying to send Nan abroad. She countered with protestations of devotion and the revelation of her delicate condition. I do not doubt that McKean testified truthfully when he repeated Nan's yarn about her pregnancy. It was a naïve and desperate gamble.

Then the Youngs moved to Sheepshead Bay, and on June third Caesar broke the news to Nan that he was sailing for Europe the following day. She undoubtedly had anticipated something of the sort, but this had the ring of finality. She refused to believe it, but he assured her that he was not joking. Nan knew, Julia knew, and Morgan knew that unless something dramatic and drastic were done, when the *Germanic* sailed at nine-thirty the following morning the battle would be lost.

Here was where the flamboyant, adolescent and boozy imagination of J. Morgan Smith came into play. Smith was an adventurer and, I believe, an unscrupulous one. He had been obliged to leave school, it will be recalled, because of "certain irregularities." He had boasted of a nonexistent relationship to J. P. Morgan. And it will also be remembered that he had turned up in San Francisco some years before with wild stories of having been shanghaied aboard a whaling vessel, of escaping, of being shipwrecked, and of having fought the natives in the Philippines, all of which has the sound of fantasy.

I believe that the crazy plot that was hatched at the news

of Young's imminent departure had been germinating in the alcoholic brain of Morgan Smith for several days before June fourth. To carry out his scheme he had to have a revolver, and the logical place to buy a revolver was in a pawnshop.

The Smiths and Nan were going to the races on June third, and the most direct route was from the St. Paul Hotel at 60th Street, down Sixth Avenue, and across 34th Street to the Long Island ferry. The Smiths did not regularly travel in cabs as Caesar Young did; Morgan had been a patron of Hyman Stern's establishment. What could be more convenient than to get off the streetcar at 34th Street, walk down four blocks to the pawnshop, buy the gun, and then return to 34th Street and take the crosstown car over to the ferry? I fancy that Julia went into the shop with her husband while Nan waited outside.

On the way home from the track that afternoon Nan told her sister and brother-in-law that it was true that Caesar was sailing the following morning and that he was calling her up to meet him that night. This was the showdown—the call to action. When they arrived at the St. Paul Hotel, Morgan explained his plan, and later, at dinner at Healy's, they continued the discussion.

"Listen, Nan," I can imagine him saying, "you've got to go through with this. Sure, it's a desperate measure, but we're in a desperate fix. If Caesar sails tomorrow you're through. But he won't leave you in the lurch when he sees that you love him so much you'd rather kill yourself than lose him."

"But I don't want to shoot myself," Nan protested.

"Don't worry. Caesar won't let you. He'll grab that gun away from you before you get a chance to use it. If it goes off in the air by accident, so much the better. The police will detain him as a witness and he won't be able to sail tomorrow morning."

Nan resisted the idea. "I won't do it!" she declared.

"You have to do it," Smith replied.

She was still resisting when she and her brother-in-law went over to Healy's the second time to get Young's telephone message, and this gives plausibility to the story of the newsboy, Hewitt. It is quite possible that he was mistaken about seeing them come out of Pabst's; it may have been Healy's, six blocks away. Hewitt could easily have been wrong about the time. Smith's angry declaration, "You have to do it!" and Nan's stubborn refusal, "I won't!" fit into the scenario.

Mr. Rand pointed out that pawnbrokers do not sell loaded revolvers, and that sometime that evening Smith had to buy bullets. Rand suggested that they were bought when Nan and Smith made their second visit to Healy's that evening.

At any rate, I believe that when Nan met Young late that night at the El station at 140th Street she had a loaded revolver in her handbag. It had to be loaded. Young was a strong man and it was part of the plot that he would wrest it from her when she attempted to use it. If he found that Nan had been threatening suicide with an empty gun, her theatrical stratagem would be transparently clear and that would be the end of everything. The gun had to be loaded.

A circumstance that persuades me that Nan had the gun in her bag that night was her statement that when Young gave her a hundred dollars—five twenty-dollar bills—she put them in her stocking because her bag was too crowded. Crowded with what? It is absurd to say that there was no room to squeeze in five bills, but it is not absurd to say that she didn't dare to open her bag in the cab in Central Park for fear that Young might see what was in it.

It was part of Morgan Smith's melodramatic scenario that Nan was to put on her act that night. Neither he nor Nan could then have anticipated that she would see Young again the following morning, and that she would ride downtown in a cab with him. Clearly if it were to be done it had to be done that night. But Nan did not draw her gun that night. Why?

It is quite evident to me that she did not want to go through with the plot, and we have her own word for it that Young, during their ride in the park, kept protesting his devotion to her and assuring her that he would send for her and that the separation would be only a brief one, hardly a propitious prelude to a melodramatic suicide attempt. But what really prevented Nan from going through with the scheme, we can be positive, was that that hour's ride around Central Park in a hansom cab was a passionately amorous one. This was Caesar Young's last opportunity to be alone with his mistress before embarking upon a protracted vacation with his attractive but, I suspect, more frigid spouse. We can be certain that Caesar did not neglect his opportunity. Those hansom cabs were conveniently suited for dalliance. When the cab pulled up before the saloon on 125th Street Nan's chance for histrionics was gone.

I am puzzled as to why Young asked Luce to meet him at all that night, but it is certain that he wanted that last sentimental hour alone with Nan before the meeting. When the cab arrived at McKeever's saloon, her opportunity to stage her attempted suicide was gone, since she certainly could not put on her act in the presence of Luce and the bartenders. But I believe that before they left the cab, Young had promised her that he would telephone to her in the morning and drive down to the pier with her.

Luce undoubtedly heard more and remembered more than he testified to. It was just too pat that he should have heard Nan's angry threats and nothing else. I have little doubt that the scene between Nan and Young in the saloon was a stormy one. The passionate glow of that last ride in the hansom cab was wearing off under the influence of many drinks and Nan's frantic realization that the zero hour was drawing near. And Caesar Young, we know, could be pretty nasty when in liquor. But Nan realized, when they parted that night, that she was seeing him again in a few hours.

As Michael's hansom cab the following morning moved relentlessly through the cobbled streets, downtown toward the pier, Nan knew that time was running out. The two stops on the way, at the hat store and at the saloon, were agonizing respites that served only to heighten the dramatic suspense. As the cab pulled away from the saloon she knew that the time had come. The steamship pier was a short distance away. In her black handbag was a loaded revolver.

Her nerves were at the breaking point; she must have been bordering on hysteria at that moment. Nan was no actress but we know that she was a girl addicted to the romantic fiction of the day, and it is easy to believe that there was poignant realism in her cry, "Caesar, I can't let you go! If you leave me life is not worth living! I would rather die than live without you!" It may be that in her overwrought condition she thought she meant it. She unsnapped her bag and drew the revolver.

There was a struggle as Young, seeing the revolver in her hand, rose from his seat and attempted to wrest it from her.

And here is a circumstance that all along I have thought important: the flaps of the hansom cab were open! He could not have stood up had the doors been closed, but with the doors open it was natural for him to rise and bend over her as he struggled to grab the gun from her hand. Then came the loud report of a pistol and Caesar toppled over across her lap.

It is impossible to reconstruct the details of the struggle, to determine the positions they were in, and to ascertain just how the trigger was pulled. Nan, I am sure, remained seated and Young was bending over her as he finally wrested the gun from her hand. This would explain the curious point of entry and the course of the bullet. It would explain, too, the black marks that Dr. O'Hanlon saw on Young's fingers that he said were powder marks.

Caesar Young lay sprawled across his mistress' lap. His left arm was about her waist; not, as it was later suspected, as an indication of an affectionate embrace, but where he had been holding her in that last death struggle. No one can ever know the horror, the terror, in Nan's mind at that moment. This catastrophe was not according to the script written by J. Morgan Smith. Her first reaction—fifteen seconds after the shot was fired—was to push open the trap in the roof and exclaim to the cab driver, "For God's sake, drive to a drugstore!"

As they drove to the drugstore one thought pounded insistently through her panic-stricken brain. The pistol! The pistol must be gotten rid of. It would never do to have them discover that she had brought it with her into the cab. It lay on the floor where it had fallen from Caesar Young's lifeless fingers. She picked it up and dropped it into the coat pocket of the body that lay prostrate across her lap. I cannot believe that this was a deliberately conscious act. Rather, I suspect, it was the automatic response of a stunned woman to that insistent "The pistol" beating in her brain. The handle of her handbag had been broken, as she revealingly said later, "in the excitement." Her white gloves still lay as she had placed them, neatly folded across her knees.

Nan, as Levy said, was no Clara Morris, no Rachel, no Ristori, nor even a Mrs. Leslie Carter, but she did not need to be. She was not acting during that agonizing drive to the hospital as she wrung her hands and kept sobbing over and over again, "Caesar, Caesar, what have you done?" Her emotions were mixed—grief, shock and, above all, fear.

In the cab on the way to the hospital Nan told Officer Junior that she had seen no gun and that she didn't know where it was. By the time she was taken, later in the morning, before Captain Sweeney, she had gotten a grip on herself. She realized the predicament she was in and that, if the pistol were traced to her and Morgan Smith, she would be in serious danger. She told Captain Sweeney that she had looked for the gun in the cab and had found it in Young's pocket.

It is evident that Morgan Smith's horror, when he heard what had happened, was as genuine as Nan's. His fantastic scheme had gone tragically awry. "Morgan did not say anything," Detective Quinn testified, "but he stood still like that and the muscles of his jaw contracted as if he were stunned. . . . He turned yellow, almost green."

But there was still a strong possibility that the truth might not come out. The newspapers from the start were speaking of Young's death as suicide and the evidence pointed to it. Nan was the only eyewitness and as soon as she got control over herself, after a night's rest in the Tombs, she stuck steadfastly to the story of suicide. If only the pistol were not traced, and there was a chance that it might not be, Nan and the Smiths would be safe.

It was the startling announcement a few days later that the pistol had been bought in Hyman Stern's pawnshop that precipitated the crisis. That night Morgan and Julia fled. They no doubt thought that they were helping Nan, but their primary motive, I believe, was to save their own skins. They were in this situation pretty deep.

The key witness in the case was Hyman Stern and I agree with Rand that he was honest and truthful. If Morgan Smith had not run away, if the pawnbroker had confronted him a few days after the shooting, the chances are that Stern might have remembered him. But nearly a year passed before Smith and Stern came face to face, and by that time the pawnbroker's recollection undoubtedly had faded. Stern was an honorable man and a nearsighted one. He may have had his suspicion about Smith, that I cannot know, but, in a case that could have meant a woman's liberty or even life, he hesitated to make a positive identification unless he was absolutely certain. Rand knew this, and I think that is why he asked Stern whether Smith looked like the man rather than, Was he the man?

The case was tried in a masterful manner by both sides. Ordinarily the prosecution in a criminal trial has most of the advantages, but owing to the peculiar facts this was not entirely so in this case. Rand had a difficult task but it would have been less difficult had it not been for the skill and alertness with which his opponent invoked the exclusionary rules of evidence against him. In a great measure Nan owed her freedom to what was kept out of the record.

Rand was committed to a theory of murder in the first

degree and he was therefore required, since he had the burden of proof, to satisfy the jury beyond any reasonable doubt that Nan had killed Young with deliberation and premeditation; that when she entered the cab on that morning she intended to take Young's life.

This, it seems to me, was almost an impossible task. I am sure that Rand would have been satisfied with a conviction of a lower degree of homicide, but it seems to me that he had to be consistent and hold out for a first-degree verdict. When he declared that Young was "a man marked for slaughter" he imposed an insuperable handicap upon himself. But it would have been dangerous for him to have argued that the killing was committed in the heat of passion. The purchase of the gun the day before and its presence in the cab made that implausible. And had he conceded the possibility of an accident he would have been out of court.

Levy was in the advantageous position of not being obliged to prove anything. His task was to create doubts in the minds of the jurors, and that he did superbly. This was a case of circumstantial evidence, and the rule in such case is that the circumstances must exclude every reasonable hypothesis except that of guilt. Otherwise the defendant has to be acquitted.

The defense did not have to convince the jury that the shooting had occurred in a particular way. All that Levy needed to do was to suggest possible alternative theories so as to create doubts in the minds of the jurors. He had one other decided advantage. Rand had to win all twelve of the jurors; his adversary needed to instill a reasonable doubt in the minds of only one or two.

The greatest weakness in Rand's case was that he was unable

to prove any conceivable motive for killing. Proof of motive is not an essential ingredient in a homicide, but in a case of circumstantial evidence it can be the determining factor. Nan had no possible reason for wanting Young to die. On the contrary, she had every reason on earth for wanting him to live.

Rand had staked his case upon his theory of murder in the first degree. Levy undoubtedly knew that there was little likelihood that the jury would condemn Nan to die in the electric chair. But there was a grave possibility that she might be found guilty of a lesser degree of homicide, which could mean a long term in prison.

With all the earnestness he was capable of, he concluded his summing up with a plea that there should be no compromise verdict.

In spite of the plea of the district attorney for a murder verdict, it turned out that not one of the twenty-four jurors who passed upon Nan's fate voted for murder in any degree. Ten voted for manslaughter and fourteen for not guilty.

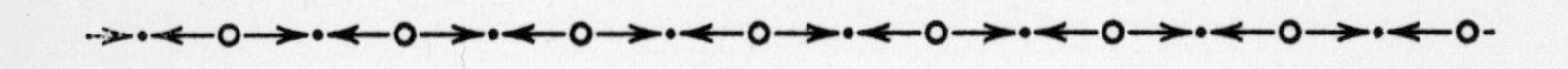

About the Author

NEWMAN LEVY is eminently well qualified to write about Nan Patterson on two counts. First, he is the son of Nan's defense counsel. Second, he is himself an expert in criminal law.

Mr. Levy was admitted to the bar in 1912. From 1916 to 1920 he served as assistant district attorney in the County of New York, and he has been a prominent trial lawyer for nearly half a century.

A lawyer and a writer of distinction, Mr. Levy's books include Opera Guyed and other volumes of light verse. His autobiography, My Double Life, was published in the spring of 1958.